Robert Smith has brought to the writing of baseball history the rare combination of literacy and a knowledge of the game's past. That a gifted novelist should possess the first of these two qualifications is not surprising; more impressive is his allegiance to accuracy.

Tom Meany, Frank Graham and Arthur Mann are a few who have similarly combined smooth technique with a reverence for facts, but they have all been actively connected with the major league scene. Smith writes from the point of view of a fan and exhibits the best qualities of that breed—compassion, constant wonder and a sort of sweet nostalgia. But he can let the irony flow, and if the occasion warrants, he can be mordant.

Until now the careers of the hundred and one men elected to the Hall of Fame have not been examined as carefully as one might think. Their obvious deeds have been recounted in various books, some better than others; but here I think is a shrewd peek at their personalities. There is proper awe, but the maple syrup has been eliminated.

This is a book that the reader will want to finish in one sitting and then return to, again and again, for refreshment.

LEE ALLEN, Historian
National Baseball Hall of Fame and Museum
Cooperstown, New York.

BASEBALL'S
HALL OF FAME
BY ROBERT SMITH

BANTAM BOOKS · TORONTO · NEW YORK · LONDON

Dedicated to
Paul C. Kelly, my favorite Father-in-Law

BASEBALL'S HALL OF FAME

A Bantam Book / published April 1965

Library of Congress Catalog Card Number: 65-17648

All rights reserved.

Copyright © 1965 by Bantam Books, Inc.

Published simultaneously in the United States and Canada.

Bantam Books are published by Bantam Books, Inc., a subsidiary of Grosset & Dunlap, Inc. Its trade-mark consisting of the words "Bantam Books" and the portrayal of a bantam, is registered in the United States Patent Office and in other countries. Marca Registrada. Bantam Books, Inc., 271 Madison Avenue, New York 16, N.Y. Printed in the United States of America

CONTENTS

Boston-Philadelphia at Boston, 1872. Standing: 4th from left, Anson; 8th, Spalding; 9th, G. Wright; 11th, H. Wright. O'Rourke is at Spalding's feet.

THE EARLY DAYS

IN THE BEGINNING, BASEBALL WAS CALLED THE "NEW YORK" GAME BECAUSE IT WAS PLAYED EXCLUSIVELY BY NEW YORK GENTLEMEN'S CLUBS. BUT IT WAS SOON IMITATED, AND AFTER THE CIVIL WAR SPREAD ACROSS THE NATION. A GENTLE GAME AT FIRST, BASEBALL BECAME ROWDY AND ROUGH WHEN SPECTATORS DEMANDED IT.

MORGAN G. BULKELEY as a baseball player, was strictly a "muffin"—the name given in baseball's earliest days to a man who played the game ineptly and entirely for fun, as a golf "duffer" plays golf. His presence in Baseball's Hall of Fame is due entirely to his year of service as first president of the National League, through the season of 1876.

Before that, Bulkeley had been president of the Hartford Dark Blues of the old National Association, one of the best of the early professional teams. And all his life he had been a famous baseball "krank"—the Dutch term used in the last

Morgan G. Bulkeley   Alexander Joy Cartwright

century to mean "fan."

In Bulkeley's day, there were not more than a few score professional ballplayers in the whole country. Boston's team, with Harry Wright and A. G. Spalding, had the best of them and Bulkeley had some of the others in Hartford. His team was so little appreciated there, however, that after the Association folded up, the Dark Blues were playing their "home" games in Brooklyn.

When William Hulbert of Chicago joined with A. G. Spalding to create the National League, they forced the organization down the throats of the eastern clubs, who could either join or see their players hired away from them. To salve eastern pride, after the League had been formed, Hulbert and Spalding agreed to let Bulkeley serve as president. After one season, Hulbert himself took over and in some books is still listed as the "first" president of the National League.

ALEXANDER JOY CARTWRIGHT the man

who invented the "New York" game of baseball, never earned any fame as a player. When he and his playmates on Murray Hill, in New York City, first worked out the diamond in a

"Father" Henry Chadwick

Arthur "Candy" Cummings

vacant lot, about 1845, there were organized teams that played town ball (a roughhouse form of rounders) while other young men, who did not play cricket, played cat-ball, which was the poor man's version of the great British game. (Cat was short for catapult—a stick used to propel the ball out of a ring while players tried to see how many bases they could touch before it was recovered. One-hole cat was cat-ball played with one "hole"—a spot for grounding the bat, like the crease in cricket.)

Cartwright thought town ball, which permitted the plug-

Old-Timers' Game at Fenway Park, Boston, 1908, with A. G. Spalding seated, 6th from left, above. Below, 2nd from right, sits inventor of catcher's mask, Fred Thayer of Harvard. Tyng of Harvard, who first wore mask, seated 6th from left below.

ging of the runner with the small hard ball, was too rowdy, while cat-ball was rather too childish. His game combined some of the features of each, with a few ideas of his own. When it was first played, the number on each side was never set—it might be 6 and it might be a dozen. The game was played until one side or another, in even innings, had scored 21 "aces" or runs. But when it was formalized by the New York Knickerbockers, Cartwright's club, there were nine men to a side. The baseline distance of 42 paces has remained almost the same until today, and most of Cartwright's other notions are retained. The 9-inning idea, however, was borrowed from the Philadelphia version of town ball.

Before Knickerbocker baseball had made even half a stride toward becoming the National Game, Cartwright was off to Hawaii, where he lived out his long life, and where he was teaching his game to natives and to haole children before many people in the States had ever heard about it.

HENRY CHADWICK before baseball awarded the title to Abner Doubleday, was known throughout the land as "Father of Baseball." The title seemed to have grown upon him by common consent and many an old-time ballplayer always referred to him as "Father" Chadwick.

He had not, of course, invented the game at all. But he nourished it when it was new, and he remained loyal to it all his life. He even played the organized game for a season (with the Washington Nationals) and in 1858 he wrote the first rule book. He invented a shorthand method of keeping score (a method that was soon outmoded) and for many a season he acted as senior authority of the game, interpreter of rules, adviser, consultant, critic—and reporter of the game. He wrote for some of the earliest sports periodicals in the nation, covering cricket and football as well as baseball. But baseball was always the game he felt closest to.

British-born, Chadwick never failed to emphasize the British origin of the game and he tried, vainly, to conserve in the game some of the British amateur tradition. He was not opposed to professionalism, however. Indeed he welcomed it as far preferable to the hypocrisy of pretending that ballplayers took no pay. He was a determined foe of corruption and of organized gambling in the game. In all the baseball "guides" and "handbooks" that he edited, he argued for clean living and honest sport. The model baseball player, he once wrote, "plays the game throughout, whether winning or losing, to the best of his ability, and retires from the field apparently content with the result, whatever it may be."

WILLIAM ARTHUR CUMMINGS has been named the inventor of the curve ball. But in his day, right after the Civil War, several of the great pitchers threw curves. All Arthur Cummings did was to find out what caused a ball to curve and set out to control it.

Like all full-time ballplayers of his day, "Candy" was an "amateur," even though he earned most of his living by playing ball. But, when baseball was new, it was deemed shameful for a man to play it for money, so the great amateur clubs (like so many of today's colleges) recruited their athletes by assuring them of undercover payment, or jobs without work.

Candy, born in Massachusetts, was throwing clamshells across the backyard of his new home in Brooklyn when the idea of curving a baseball came to him. He practiced with a nickel baseball until he found out what caused the ball to dip or break; and soon after that he joined a teen-age ball club (Arthur was 14) and became their star.

Candy Cummings finally turned openly professional. He pitched for the New York Mutuals (Bill Tweed's team), for Baltimore, for the "old" Philadelphia Athletics, with the Hartford Dark Blues and the Cincinnati Reds, where he ended his career. Eventually there were many pitchers who could out-curve and outthrow him. But he remained the most famous of them all.

ALBERT GOODWILL SPALDING for all practical purposes, invented the National League and so is largely responsible for the health and longevity of the professional game. His name is still imprinted on the baseballs used by the National League—but that is because he founded the company that manufactures the balls.

Hurley, Sub.; G. Wright, S.S.; Allison, C.; McVey, R.F; Leonard, L.F.
Sweasy, 2d B.; Waterman, 3d B.; H. Wright, C.F.; Brainard, P.; Gould, 1st B.

RED STOCKING B. B. CLUB OF CINCINNATI.

Spalding (left) swings bat in 1908 Old-Timers' game. He chooses up sides (right) in old style by fitting fingers on bat. (Top) picture shows first pro team.

Al Spalding originally rose to fame as the kid pitcher of the Forest City nine, from Rockford, Illinois, the first team to win from the supposedly unbeatable Washington Nationals during the first great baseball tour in 1867. Al was just 16 years old then, a lanky, long-armed, but graceful young man with a fiery underhand pitch. He went on from there to Boston, where Harry Wright formed a professional team, after the Cincinnati Red Stockings had folded up. With the Boston .Red Stockings, Spalding became a national figure. His first season he pitched 30 complete games, and won 20 of them. Next year, he won 36, and the next year after that, he won 41, then 52, then 56. He might have gone on getting better and better, but the National Association (which was the only professional league then) was suffering from lack of patronage, from the influence of gamblers, and from the inability of most batters in the league to hit Al Spalding's pitches.

Rather than let his job fold under him, Spalding interested a Chicago fan, William Hulbert, in starting a new league, where there would be strict control of gambling and enforcement of contracts. The National League was born in 1876, with Spalding managing the Chicago club. He celebrated the new league by pitching 61 complete games that year and winning 47. That was his last season as a pitcher. Next year he played first and second base and in 1879 he turned over the manager's job to Cap Anson.

Spalding was president of the Chicago club from 1890 to 1891 and led the club owners in the struggle against the Players' Brotherhood in 1890. At the end of the century he waged a valiant fight against "syndicate" baseball and won that too. Meanwhile his sporting goods firm prospered. He began to publish the official guides and record books for the major leagues and supplied most of the official equipment. He even wrote the first complete history of the National Game (or had it written under his name).

At nearly every major turn in baseball's history the name of Albert Spalding stood out: in the first national tour in 1867; in the first one-hit game ever pitched (June 27, 1871); in the first baseball trip to England, 1874; in the beginning of the first permanent league; in the adoption of the first "official" ball; even in the name of the first 200-game winner: A. G. Spalding himself.

GEORGE WRIGHT before there was any such thing as "organized" baseball, was playing the game for a living. Born in 1847, in Harlem, New York (now a part of New York City), just two years after the game was invented, George began to play the "New York" game of ball as a boy. He played ball first for the Gotham club in New York when he was 17 years old, put in a season with the Philadelphia Olympics in 1865, then came back to play for the Gothams and the Morrisania Unions.

When brother Harry, who had gone to Cincinnati as a cricket professional, decided in 1869 to create an openly professional baseball club there, George was one of the first men hired and the highest-priced man on the team ($1400).

George could play everywhere on a ball club and at one time

George Wright, age 25

Brother Harry, age 37

or another tried every position. He liked shortstop best, however, and for a long time he was the best in the country at that position. He played barehanded of course and used to bring cheers by his boldness in spearing hot line drives (the ball then was far livelier than the modern ball). He was one of the first shortstops to cover second base when the second baseman had been drawn off the bag, and he ranged right and left to back up other players as few of his contemporaries ever did.

He made 304 hits out of 483 times at bat with the Red Stockings in 1869, with 49 home runs. By the time he entered the National Association, however, the ball had been deadened. Still, he hit well over .300 for four of his first five years in Boston.

When the National League was formed, George played with Boston, then managed the Providence club for a season, came back to Boston as shortstop in 1880 and finished his career in Providence in 1882. Meanwhile he had founded the Boston sporting goods firm of Wright and Ditson.

WILLIAM HENRY WRIGHT is properly

called the father of professional baseball, for he organized and captained (in those days the field manager was the captain) the first openly professional team in baseball's history: the Cincinnati Red Stockings. He also established the first professional team in Boston (called the Reds), after the Red Stockings had disbanded, and the brought his team into the first professional league, the National Association.

Born in England, Harry as a youth served as a cricket professional with St. George's Cricket Club, who played their games on the Elysian Fields at Hoboken, New Jersey, where the first baseball club, the Knickerbockers of New York, also played. Harry learned the game there and took his knowledge to Cincinnati. His Red Stockings became National Champions in 1869. Harry was an outfielder then, but, when his kid brother George was not playing shortstop, Harry could fill in there and he occasionally took a turn as pitcher. When the league was formed, and Harry was manager of Boston, he continued to play regularly and remained in the line-up for 4 seasons. He played 1 game a season for the next 4 years, just to keep his hand in. But it was as an organizer and a manager that Harry made his deepest mark on the game.

He offered his counsel free to people from all over the country who were interested in starting baseball teams, and no one can count the number of baseball diamonds that were laid out as he patiently suggested, the number of ball clubs that were organized in accordance with his detailed advice, or the number of down-and-out players who were indebted to his kindness.

William Henry (Harry) Wright in 1872 led the first pro team in Boston. His shoes were old-fashioned even then.

The Providence Club in 1884 where Radbourne, far left, earned name "Old Hoss" by accepting full burden when Sweeney, left, holding ball, walked out on team.

OLD CENTURY

ONCE BASEBALL BECAME PROFESSIONAL. EQUIPMENT, SUCH AS THE GLOVE AND MASK, WERE INVENTED AND RULES WERE OFTEN RADICALLY CHANGED. THE OVER-HAND THROW SUPERSEDED THE UNDERHAND TOSS, THE BUNTED BALL REPLACED THE "FAIR-FOUL HIT," COMBINATION PLAYS WERE DEVISED. THE PITCHING DISTANCE WAS LENGTHENED—AND BASEBALL BECAME SIMILAR TO THE GAME KNOWN TODAY

ADRIAN CONSTANTINE ANSON was called "Cap" (the manager of a team in the old days was always named the "captain"). When he first entered professional ball. with the Forest City team of Rockford, Illinois (where A. G. Spalding made his start earlier), he was known as "Baby" Anson, or "the Marshalltown Infant." He had been the first white child born in Marshalltown, Iowa, and he played his first baseball there on a team made up almost entirely of his father and brothers. Twenty-seven years later, when Anson ended his big-league career, he was known as "Pop," for he was one of the oldest men still active in the game.

Anson was a mighty hitter all his life. As a first baseman, he was noted chiefly for his ability to stretch his 6-foot frame an extra inch or so to snag a high throw that seemed impossible for him to reach. As a manager, he was notorious as a rough-tongued "coacher" and bullier of umpires, opponents, and even fans. But as a batsman, he struck terror to the hearts of pitchers even when he was deemed too old to play. His hits were usually booming drives, streaking on a dead-level course to the outfield. He hit the ball where it was pitched and his drives might land in any field.

Anson was supposed to have invented, or at least to have been one of the first to practice the hit-and-run play. He stood loosely in the box, never setting his feet until the pitch was coming, and then he might choke up or swing the full length of his bat. He was a proud man and religious about his physical condition. In a day when most ballplayers ate and drank as heartily as they could afford to, Big Anse ate no fried foods, drank no strong drink, did not smoke, and avoided potatoes and sweets.

As manager of the Chicago team, Cap Anson won a devoted following who stuck to him no matter what the fortunes of the team. At last he became Pop Anson to his players and to his fans, and when he had to leave Chicago at last, his team was long known as "the Orphans."

DENNIS BROUTHERS from 1881 through 1885, was the hero of every small boy in Buffalo, New York, where he played first base for the Buffalo team of the National

Cap Anson after he ''jumped'' to Chicago, 1876.

Big Dan Brouthers hit a long ball for Detroit.

League. (He also played outfield and third base once or twice and pitched a little too.) Big Dan was the mightiest batsman of that day, a man who believed in swinging the full length of his heavy warclub and who could belt even a wild pitch beyond the most distant outfielder.

In his five seasons at Buffalo he never once hit for an average of less than .318 and his long home runs and mighty doubles were the talk of the town for years. When he and three of his teammates (Rowe, White, and Richardson), making up Buffalo's "Big Four," were sold to Detroit for $8000 in 1885 the transaction was a thing to marvel at. In Detroit, he continued to hit well above .300, as he did for 14 consecutive seasons in big-league ball. His high mark of .419 in 1887 was topped only by the great Cap Anson of Chicago. His lifetime average in the majors was .348.

Big Dan—6 feet 2, and 200 pounds, with a mighty mustache to go with his outsize frame—started and finished his career playing bush-league ball in and around Poughkeepsie, New York. Beginning his major league career with Troy, in the National League, he played with Buffalo, Detroit, Boston, Brooklyn, Baltimore, Louisville, and Philadelphia—and even came back in 1904, when he was 46 years old, to play 2 games with John McGraw's New York Giants. In every city he left memories of mighty wallops.

JESSE CAIL BURKETT one of the greatest batters of all time, was a pitcher when he joined the New York Giants in 1890. He won 1 game and lost 12, but he batted for .309. From that time forth, except for a season in St. Louis 12 years later when he pitched 1 game and lost it, and played some at shortstop and third base, he was an outfielder, and a great one. Only two other hitters (Ty Cobb and Rogers Hornsby) attained a batting average of .400 or better as often as Burkett did. He did it three times: 1895, 1896, and 1899.

Burkett was a small man, only 5 feet 8 inches tall. But he was fast and strong, an excellent bunter, and, batting left-handed as he did, quick to get down to first base.

Most of his days were spent in organized baseball. He became a professional at the age of sixteen in Scranton, Pennsylvania, and after 15 years in the majors (with New York, Cleveland, St. Louis, and Boston) he bought the minor league ball club in Worcester, Massachusetts, managed it, and played on it for 7 years. After that, he managed other minor league teams, scouted for the New York Giants, coached baseball at Holy Cross College, and in 1933, when he was 63 years old, was manager of the Lowell team in the New England League.

Jesse "Crab" Burkett

John Gibson Clarkson

In his 16 years in the majors, Jesse Burkett only five times hit for less than .300. His best year was 1895, when he won the championship with an average of .423.

As a batting coach, Jesse Burkett had but one secret to impart to his charges: the indispensable quality in a batter was "that old confeedience." Jesse had it to spare.

JOHN GIBSON CLARKSON was known all his life (a tragically short one) as a moody and sensitive young man. It required the tenderest handling to keep him pitching. Yet when he was on the mound there were few of his day who could match him.

Clarkson broke into the National League in 1882 before he

had turned 21, becoming a pitcher for the Worcester team in his native state of Massachusetts. He won only 1 game out of 3 with this club and found himself next season with Saginaw of the Northwestern League. In his second season there he struck out 339 in 40 games. Before the year was out he was back in the National League, this time with Cap Anson's Chicago White Stockings. He completed the 1884 season there by winning 10 of the 14 games he pitched while striking out 96. Anson thought handsome John was the best pitcher he had ever seen, but soon discovered that if Clarkson was scolded he could not pitch at all while, if the manager remembered to praise him, John would go out and pitch 6 games in a row.

In 1885 Clarkson had his finest year with the White Stockings. He appeared in 70 games, won 53 of them and lost only 16. He struck out 318. In July of that year he shut out Providence 4 to 0, allowing not a single hit. In 1886 Clarkson won 36 games out of 53, and the next season he won 38 out of 58. Then he was sold to Boston for $10,000, the same price the great "King" Kelly had commanded from the same club a year before. Now Clarkson and Kelly became the $20,000 battery and John began to win games for Boston: 33 in 1888, 49 in 1889, 26 in 1890, 34 in 1891, and 24 in 1892. He was not a strong-arm pitcher but strictly a curve-ball man. He had such strength in his long fingers that he could spin a billiard ball so it would run a complete circle on a table.

Clarkson, who was used to pitching day after day (in 1889 he pitched 2 games in 1 day and later went to the mound 8 days in a row), began to fade in 1892. His arm was sore and discouragement took much of the starch out of him. Boston released him and Cleveland signed him. But John never regained his form. He appeared in 34 games for Cleveland in 1893 and won 16 while losing 18. Next year his record was 8 and 8. He found it difficult to finish a game these days and was given to moods of black despair. He had been posting more bases on balls than strike-outs for the past few seasons and it came to him at last that his career was over. He went home despondent. He was committed to a mental hospital before he died and never fully recovered his sanity.

CHARLES ALBERT COMISKEY made his great contribution to the game by playing his first-base position wide and deep, ranging into the outfield, or up toward second, to catch flies or gather ground balls. In an age when basemen were closely anchored to their bags, this play created a sensation.

With the St. Louis Browns, Comiskey four times won the "National Championship" and completely revolutionized infield play by teaching all his infielders to back each other up, to shift positions according to the tactical situation, even to

The "Old Roman," Comiskey   Hugh Duffy

drop back into the "outfield" to smother hard-hit balls. He was the first too to bring the pitcher over to first on a ball hit to the first baseman.

Comiskey, who was named the "Noblest Roman" by a sports writer, eventually became the "Old Roman," for he stayed in baseball all his life. He helped organize the American League and took over the Chicago franchise—a property that eventually became worth millions. The park he built to house his great Chicago teams still boasts of its "Bards' Room," where Comiskey's cronies, who called themselves "the Woodland Bards," used to gather after games, or in between, to drink and sing and celebrate the joys of baseball.

HUGH DUFFY who still holds the highest batting average ever recorded in the major leagues since the modern pitching distance was adopted (.438 in 1894), got his major league start in Chicago but earned his greatest fame in Boston, where he was one of the Heavenly Twins of the Boston Beaneaters' outfield. (Tommy McCarthy was the other.) A stumpy little Irishman who could run like a rabbit, he belted the ball heavily wherever he played. In 16 active seasons in four different major leagues, he only four times fell below .300 at the plate.

Born in Rhode Island, he spent most of his career in New England and stayed in baseball all his life. He was only 17 when he turned professional, as a catcher with Hartford in the Eastern League. He was still a scout for the Boston Red Sox when he was 84. In between, he played for Springfield and Salem (Massachusetts) in the minor leagues, then signed with the Chicago National League club in 1888. When the Brotherhood strike came in 1890, Hugh Duffy, like most of the stars of the day, jumped to the Players' League, then moved to Boston in the American Association and stayed in Boston when the Association was merged with the National League in 1892.

Duffy had a batting style much like that employed by Mel Ott in a later era, except that Duffy hit right-handed. Duffy too would lift his forward foot when he began his swing. Although he was (according to Cap Anson, Duffy's first major league manager) too short and too light to be a major leaguer, he had a mighty pair of shoulders and the balls he hit would travel like rifle shots.

Hugh Duffy became a manager when his playing days were nearly done, taking charge of Milwaukee, the Philadelphia Nationals, Providence, the Chicago White Sox, Milwaukee again, the Portland (Maine) team, Toronto, and the Boston Red Sox in 1921 and 1922, with time between and afterward spent in scouting. Active with the Red Sox almost to the day of his death, he would never tell his age in his later years.

William (Buck) Ewing,
wore two gloves
while catching for
the N. Y. Giants
in the 1880's.
Note old
side-buckle belt.

6. FROM LEFT TO RIGHT, THE PLAYERS ARE (TOP ROW) HART, McFARLAND, DAVIS, PRESIDENT COMISKEY, ISBEL
AN AND WHITE. (MIDDLE ROW) WALSH, SMITH, ROTH, HAHN, DUNDON, DONOHUE, O'NEILL, TANNEHILL AND ROH
(BOTTOM ROW) TOWNE, ALTROCK, OWEN, PATTERSON, DOUGHERTY, JONES AND FIENE.

IGHT 1906
BURKE

AMERICAN LEAGUE CHAMPIONS

The champion Chicago
White Sox, owned by
Comiskey, beat
the Chicago Cubs
in the 1906
World Series.

WILLIAM EWING was one of the best-loved professional ballplayers, by both players and fans, who ever lived. Buck, a gentle, good-natured, remarkably fleet-footed man, was probably the first catcher to throw the ball to second from a crouch. "It wastes time to straighten up," he used to explain. But it was many years before other catchers learned the wisdom of this.

Buck played his first ball with a club called the Mohawk Browns. Like most other professionals, of whom there were only a few score in his earliest days, Buck played nearly every position. He entered organized ball with the Rochester club in the National Association, then joined the great Troy Haymakers.

When the Haymakers disbanded, Buck, with most of the others, went to New York. In his first year with the Giants, Buck led the National League with 10 home runs. In 1889, except for one pitching effort, he was a full-time catcher and led the league in putouts and assists in that position.

Buck became a manager when the Players' Brotherhood League was formed and he took all the New York fans with him.

Up to the day of his death, fans in New York still talked of the day he stole second and third, then called out (he enjoyed ribbing the opponents this way) that he was about to steal home. He stole that base too with a wild dash and a mighty slide that was reproduced in a lithograph as "Ewing's Famous Slide" and sold all over town.

WILLIAM ROBERT HAMILTON stole more bases (797) than any other player who ever played in the major leagues, and scored more runs in a single season (196) than any player before or since, not excepting Cobb, Wagner, or Ruth. He made most of his base-stealing records, it is true, in the days before the catcher caught right up under the bat and before pitchers had learned not to allow baserunners to get a head start on their pitch to the plate. But Billy was one of the fastest men who ever played ball.

Playing for Kansas City in the American Association (a major league then) in 1889, Billy stole 117 bases. (Cobb's

Billy Hamilton stole 797 bases in his major-league career.

top season mark was 96.) Billy's lifetime major league total of almost a thousand stolen bases is 45 ahead of Cobb's total. And Billy played only 14 years in the majors while Cobb played 24.

Billy Hamilton did his best playing for Philadelphia of the National League, where he teamed with Big Ed Delahanty and Big Sam Thompson in the outfield. In 1894, Billy hit .398 and stole 7 bases in a single game, tying a record made by George Gore in 1881 and never reached by anyone since.

A short, solid left-handed hitter (5 feet 6, and 165 pounds), Billy had, in his 14 years of active play in the majors, only 2 seasons (his first and his last) when he hit for less than .300. His lifetime average was .344.

TIMOTHY J. KEEFE was so marvelous a pitcher for

the Giants that some fans nowadays think he was just a myth. But Tim was a very real and very mighty right-handed pitcher throughout the 1880's. Beginning in 1883, Tim Keefe, who hailed from Cambridge, Massachusetts, won 30 games or more every season for 7 seasons in a row. In 1883, pitching for the New York Metropolitans of the American Association (the original Mets), Tim won 41 games and lost 26. In 1886, pitching for the New York Giants (owned, like the Mets, by "Truthful Jeems" Mutrie), Tim won 42 games and lost but 20.

Tim's most famous feat however was his 19-game winning streak in 1888, beginning on June 23 and ending on August 10. This record stood unmatched until Rube Marquard, also of the Giants, duplicated the feat in 1912. Oddly enough, both men achieved their effectiveness through the development of a baffling change of pace—called a "slow ball" in Tim Keefe's day. Because Tim learned to throw his slow ball with the same motion he used on his fast pitch, he was able to bewilder the most famous batters of his day. Tim was fast too and his fiery speed gave extra value to his slow ball.

Tim was not a big man. He stood 5 feet 10 and weighed 185. But he was strong and durable. He pitched for amateur teams around Boston when he was in his teens, starting with the Franklin Juniors of Cambridge when he was 18 years old. When he was 19 he was pitching in Lewiston, Maine, for an amateur team called the Androscoggins, after Lewiston's river, and he pitched for several other New England amateur clubs before turning professional at the age of 23. Amateurs in Tim's day were not always strictly amateur, for there was usually an overpaid job, with no real work to it, attached to an assignment with any of the fast amateur teams of the day. Tim's professional career began with the Utica club of the National Association in 1879 and he played that same year with both New Bedford and Albany. He started the 1880 season with Albany but joined the Troy team in the National League before the season was over. He pitched his first National League game for Troy in August, 1880, beating Cincinnati 4 to 2. Tim finished his career at the age of 37 with the Phillies, for whom he won 21 games in 1892 and 10 in 1893.

WILLIAM HENRY KEELER the man who is supposed to have invented the slogan "Hit 'em where they ain't," was a .300 or better hitter almost all his major league life. Wee Willie played with the New York Giants, Baltimore, and Brooklyn in the National League and with New York in the American League.

It was in Baltimore that he attained his greatest fame, and his highest batting average: .432 in 1897. That season he hit safely in 44 consecutive games. An infielder when he started in the majors, he moved to the outfield when he came to Baltimore (after 2 seasons in New York and Brooklyn) and stayed there the rest of his career. A tiny man (5 feet 4, and 140 pounds), Willie was never a slugger but he was a master of the bunt and the "Baltimore chop"—a stroke he and his teammates perfected to bounce hits over the heads of charging infielders who were looking for a bunt. He specialized in a choked-bat swing, placing the ball carefully where the fielders had left room.

Before the rules prevented it, Willie would often tire a pitcher out by bunting balls foul, thirty or forty in a row. To Keeler, a bunt was not a sacrifice but a means of getting on base. He never gave up a "needless" out but would rely on his tremendous speed and his careful placing of the ball to get him safely to first.

Willie stayed in organized ball for 20 years, finishing his career with Toronto in the Eastern League in 1911.

Tim Keefe, the legendary
New York Giant pitcher.

Willie Keeler of New York,
Baltimore, and Brooklyn.

Boston Beaneaters in 1889 included Dan Brouthers,
3rd from left, top, Radbourne, sitting 2nd from left,
John Clarkson, next, and Mike Kelly, beside manager.

Mike Kelly, (left) was Boston's "$10,000 beauty"
when bought from Chicago in 1887. He prompted the
chant: "Slide, Kelly, on your belly! Slide, Kelly, slide!"

MICHAEL JOSEPH KELLY is a name that has lived in the language for more than a lifetime, in the catch phrase "Slide, Kelly, slide!" For Mike Kelly of Chicago and Boston was the greatest slider of his day—the inventor, it is said, of the hook slide. He was a great improviser on the field and took advantage of every loophole in the rules. Kelly was the first right fielder to move in close behind the baseline. He thought up the trick of dropping his mask on the plate, when he was catching, to discourage the runner from coming in too fast. He was (so he said) the first catcher to use finger signals to tell his pitcher what to throw and the first man to see the sense of passing these signals on to infield and out-field.

In Chicago, the fleet-footed Kelly, a strapping young man with a big black mustache, came into his own. Playing pitcher, catcher, every infield position, and the outfield, Kelly earned a devoted following.

He was sold to Boston in 1887 for $10,000 and was called, for a time, "the ten-thousand-dollar beauty." In Boston his popularity was as great as ever. He became manager there for a time, then his skill began to fade and he was sent to New York, returned to Boston, and allowed to drift into the minors.

More famous for his improvisations and for his daring base-running than for his batting or fielding, Kelly still managed to post a batting average of .315 for his years in the majors. His high mark was .394 in 1887, his first year with Boston. The year before, while with Chicago, he led the National League with an average of .388.

THOMAS FRANCIS MICHAEL McCARTHY a

little Irishman from South Boston, was a menace on the basepaths, and he and his Beaneater teammates were always scheming new ways to gain an advantage over the opponents or find a loophole in the rules. Tommy was one of the first players to learn to steal the catcher's signals, when he stood on second base, and relay them to the batter. And he was adept at the hit-and-run—still a new tactic in baseball in his day.

Studio slide by Tommy McCarthy of Boston.

Tommy, according to veteran umpire Bill Klem, was responsible for a change in the rule governing the man on base after a sacrifice fly. The rule used to state that the runner could not leave his base until the fielder held the ball in his hand. So Tommy used to keep a caught ball bounding from one hand to the other as he ran in to the infield—and of course it was then too late for the runner to try to score.

In 1888, Tommy jumped to the American Association and began to play steadily in St. Louis. That year he stole 109 bases. He tried a spot of pitching but earned no decision, and even, in 1890, served as manager for a time. In St. Louis, he was "Little Mack" or "the Kid," but he was a big man at the plate in 1890, when he batted .351 and led the league in runs scored.

Tommy finished his playing days in Brooklyn, went to scouting for Cincinnati after that, and later coached baseball at Dartmouth, Holy Cross, and Boston College.

CHARLES ARTHUR NICHOLS despite his slight stature (5 feet 9, and 135 pounds when he came to Boston in 1890), and despite the fact that the men who made the selections for the Hall of Fame did not notice him for many years, was still the greatest pitcher who ever worked for the Boston National League club. Indeed some of his records have never been matched in either league. For 7 seasons out of 8, with the Boston Beaneaters, the Kid won 30 games or more. In his lifetime in the National League, where he pitched for 15 years, for Boston, for St. Louis, and for Philadelphia, Nichols worked in 582 games and won 360 of them. (In only 20 did he fail to earn listing as the "pitcher of record.")

The Kid never objected to pitching frequently. Once he pitched 3 days in a row, in different cities (in 1892) and completed and won all 3 games.

But in the Kid's day, pitchers did not loll on the bench or snooze in the bullpen when they were not scheduled to pitch. On his "days off" Kid Nichols often had to stand at the entrance gate and keep an eye on the ticket taker, then count the tickets afterward. One day at the Polo Grounds in New York, he counted 30,000 tickets. "That was tougher than pitching nine innings," he said.

Kid Nichols had no tricky deliveries, as so many of his contemporaries had. He relied on speed, control, and change

Kid Nichols won 361.

Copyright 1887.
Goodwin & Co.

~ J. O'Rourke G. - Boston. ~

OLD JUDGE CIGARETTES Goodwin & Co., New York.

Orator Jim O'Rourke poses in a Boston studio with ball on a string.

of pace. He never even had a curve to brag about. Yet he averaged about 120 strikeouts a season for 15 years in the majors.

JAMES HENRY O'ROURKE became known as "the Orator" early in his career, because he was a well-read man who loved to talk and who could lecture his teammates, or even his employer, for hours at a time about his legal rights. Jim started playing ball with the Bridgeport Unions in Connecticut when he was 15 years old, long before he was able to grow the luxuriant mustache that later became his trade-mark. He played his last professional game when he was 63. During the intervening years he played every position on a baseball team, and sometimes played them all on the same day. He also organized and managed teams, served as president, secretary, and treasurer of the Connecticut State League, and for a time acted as groundskeeper for the team he managed. (They played their games on the O'Rourke farm in Connecticut.)

Orator Jim took part in the first National League game ever played (Boston vs. Philadelphia, April 22, 1876) and he got the first hit ever made in the league—a long single to left, where Jim almost always hit them. Jim was catcher, first baseman, and third baseman with the Boston Red Stockings before the National League was born, and after that he became an outfielder. He was not the best of fielders (he once made 5 errors in one game) but he was a powerful pull hitter who terrorized third basemen with his slashing daisycutters. Jim O'Rourke deserted the Boston team when they tried to make him pay for his own uniform and his success in jumping to Providence prompted the creation of the "reserve rule" that has been a part of baseball contracts ever since.

Jim won his widest fame as a catcher and outfielder for the New York Giants in the 80's and 90's. In 1904, when he was 52, he talked his old friend John McGraw into letting him catch one more game for the Giants, and that was his last appearance in the big leagues. He got a hit that day too.

CHARLES G. RADBOURNE became the "Old Hoss"
in a day when iron-man pitchers were commonplace. But Radbourne was the workhorse of them all. In his day, a pitcher did not leave the game when he grew unsteady: he went out to right field and played out the nine innings, for substitution was not allowed except in case of a disabling injury. But it did not weaken the team to have the Old Hoss in right field, for he was a solid hitter too and played there often when it was not his turn to pitch. Indeed, when he first took to playing baseball with the Peoria Reds (after quitting his job as railroad brakeman) he was known as a hitter and played right field regularly.

Rad's greatest year was 1884, when he won the pennant

for Providence almost singlehanded. When the other pitcher on the staff (Providence had only two regulars and one "change" pitcher) quit in a rage, Radbourne offered to shoulder the whole burden. He pitched and won 18 games in a row, lost 1, and then took 8 more, to salt away the pennant. That year he established the all-time record of 60 wins in one season. He pitched a no-hit game against Cleveland in 1883, when he won 49 games. In his 12 seasons in the major leagues (including 1 season in the Players' League) he nine times won more than 20 games.

RODERICK JOHN WALLACE a pale, angular

young man with long arms and legs, was one of the original Cleveland Spiders, the tough, long-legged, and spider-armed crew that used to scare baserunners in the National League throughout the 1890's.

But Bobby was something more than a roughneck. Starting as a pitcher in Clarion, Pennsylvania, in 1893, when he was 18 years old, he moved up quickly to Cleveland, where he was converted to a third baseman, after two mediocre seasons on the mound (or "on the points," as they said in those days). He immediately began to pound the ball hard and he remained an infielder all the rest of his career, which lasted 25 years in the big leagues. After 5 seasons in Cleveland, he moved to the St. Louis National League team and played in that city 20 years, first in the National League, then in the American League, then back to the National League again.

In 1911, he became manager of the St. Louis Browns and played less frequently. He was a defensive player mostly, and deemed the best fielder of his time. After managing for 2 seasons, he turned over the job to George Stovall, but remained on the roster as a handyman, ready to play any infield position. In 1917, he switched back to the National League to put in two seasons with the St. Louis Cardinals as shortstop, third baseman, and second baseman. He played his final big-league game in 1918, when he was 44 years old. In 1937, he came back for a year to manage the Cincinnati Reds.

Bobby was perhaps the best-paid player of his time and before he quit the game was reputed to be the wealthiest.

JOHN MONTGOMERY WARD was a Columbia Law School graduate, and after his pitching career was over he held a big-league job for 10 seasons with his bat and his brain.

When John Ward joined the Providence Club in the National League in 1878, he pitched 35 complete games for them and won 22 of them. In 1880, with the same club, he pitched a perfect game against Buffalo, winning 5 to 0 and not allowing a Buffalo man to reach first base.

Ward's best year with the bat came in 1887 after he had joined the New York Giants. He hit .371 that year, while playing shortstop, and scored 113 runs. Ward, as head of the Players' Brotherhood, led the Brotherhood Strike in 1890 and helped form the Players' League. When the strike was over, he rejoined the National League as manager of Brooklyn and led the club for 2 seasons finishing in sixth place the first year and in third place the second year. Ward then moved back to the New York Giants to finish his career, and during those years he played in only a few games himself, retiring after 1894. He returned to organized baseball in 1911 as president of the Boston Club in the National League and also served as attorney for the National League, arguing at a congressional hearing in favor of the reserve rule that had prompted the rebellion he himself had led.

Roderick (Bobby) Wallace
stayed in the majors 25 years.

The Providence team in 1879 had some of the finest players in the
league, including Captain George Wright, standing 4th from right, John
Montgomery Ward, 2nd from left, and Jim O'Rourke, reclining on right.

THE NEW

WITH THE NEW CENTURY CAME A MAJOR LEAGUE WHICH RECRUITED PLAYERS FROM SANDLOTS AND MINORS. THERE CAME ALSO THE RULING UMPIRE WHO WON THE RESPECT OF THE FANS WHO APPROVED OF A TIGHT CONTROL. THE LEAGUE PROMPTED INTER-LEAGUE CHAMPIONSHIP PLAY, LATER KNOWN AS THE WORLD SERIES, WHICH HELPED MAKE BASEBALL A BOOMING BUSINESS.

"Cousin Ed" Barrow, who never wore a big-league uniform, still became manager of Detroit Tigers, of Boston Red Sox (above, 1919) and finally general manager of New York Yankees.

CENTURY

EDWARD GRANT BARROW a man who never liked night baseball and was opposed to the "farm system" of recruiting and training players, still did a great deal to modernize the game of baseball. He was the first baseball executive to call a halt to the practice of having ushers pry away from the fans the baseballs that happened to land in the stands. He was the first to put numbers on the players' uniforms, so the fans could identify them. He was the first to mark the outfield fences to indicate the distances from home plate, so fans could amuse themselves by contemplating the length of the home runs hit by the great sluggers under Ed Barrow's command.

Barrow owned the Paterson, New Jersey, franchise when the Atlantic League was formed and here he hired, and helped develop, a rookie named Honus Wagner, whom Barrow always considered the greatest baseball player of all time. Barrow became president of the Atlantic League and in this job got himself a reputation as a circus promoter. But the stunts he pulled, he said, were out of sheer desperation. He hired a girl pitcher, used heavyweight champion Jim Corbett as first baseman a few times, and had John L. Sullivan and Jim Jeffries for umpires.

When he got to the big leagues, however, Barrow eschewed all such hippodroming, for he felt baseball by itself was all the entertainment a man needed. In 1917, he became manager of the Boston Red Sox and joined his destiny there to that of Babe Ruth—the only man who ever called Barrow "Eddie." And Eddie Barrow was one of the few men who was able to discipline the Babe. It was Barrow who decided that Ruth should become an outfielder rather than a pitcher.

After Babe Ruth went to the Yankees, Ed Barrow followed, to become business manager and eventually president. While Barrow was there, buying players, making trades, and developing rookies, the Yankees won 14 pennants and 10 World Series, and put on display a long list of the greatest ball players ever brought into the same park.

ROGER BRESNAHAN started out as a pitcher with the old Washington team in the National League. He pitched

Ed Barrow when he was president of the Eastern League in the early 1900's.

Roger Bresnahan, left, liked to pretend he was born in Ireland. Jimmy Archer, his teammate and second-string catcher on the Chicago Cubs, really was.

7 games in 1897, when he was 19 years old, and won 4 of them, but the team could not pay him the salary he wanted so he went back home to Toledo. By the time he got back to the big leagues, with Baltimore of the American League, he was both pitcher and catcher.

Bresnahan was unusually fast for a catcher and often batted first in the line-up. He was an unusually brainy player too—a schemer and a scrapper, just like John McGraw, who took Bresnahan along when he jumped from the Baltimore team to the New York Giants. In New York, Roger was a pitcher, catcher, third baseman, shortstop, outfielder, and assistant manager. He invented various stratagems for outwitting umpires and was given credit too for inventing shinguards. But all Roger did was wear his shinguards openly, while other catchers were still ashamedly concealing them beneath their stockings.

Bresnahan played in only one World Series, the 1905 Series against Philadelphia, and he was one of the few men who hit hard in those games. He had an average of .313. In his best year with the Giants he hit .350 and stole 34 bases. He was skillful at working a pitcher for a walk and often tried hard to get himself nicked by a pitch to get a free ticket to first.

Bresnahan became a manager in St. Louis and nearly won a pennant in 1911 with the Cardinals. A train wreck in mid-season seemed to take the starch out of his team, however, and they fell back into the second division. After one more vain effort to come in first, Roger resigned as manager and went to Chicago, where he played 2 seasons with the Cubs, and served 1 season as manager. He came back finally to help John McGraw as coach and ended his active career as a coach with Detroit.

MORDECAI PETER CENTENNIAL BROWN

was called "Three-Finger" Brown because he lost most of his right index finger, as a boy, when he was feeding field corn into a chopper. The loss of the gripping part of his finger gave him a natural "sinker" pitch that acted like a knuckle ball—dropping down sharply as it crossed the plate.

Brown played third base in sandlot ball and became an

able infielder. When he turned to pitching, he could still range all over the grass around his position to field ground balls. In 1908, with the Chicago Cubs, whom he pitched to a pennant that year, he accepted 108 fielding chances on the pitching mound and never made an error. (He also won 29 games that year.) In his 14 years as a major league pitcher, starting with St. Louis in the National League in 1903, Brown had only 4 losing seasons. In his great years with the Chicago Cubs, from 1904 to 1912, he had 8 winning seasons in a row, with 6 consecutive years in which he won 20 or more games.

Brown's pitch, a wide, fast-falling curve, caused most batters to top the ball badly and send it spinning out on the ground. With Brown on the mound, the Cub infield (Steinfeldt, Tinker, Evers, and Chance) became nearly impenetrable.

Brown could walk into a game without a warm-up in the late innings, get the batters out and go on to pitch nine innings in the next game. In 1908, between September 22 and the end of the World Series (which the Cubs won from Detroit) Brown pitched in 10 games within 22 days and won both ends of a double-header in that stretch.

FRANK LEROY CHANCE like many big fellows of

his day, was known as "Husk"—he was 6 feet tall and his playing weight was 190. A solid hitter and a sure-handed fielder, Chance earned most of his fame as a manager. He led the Chicago Cubs for 7½ seasons and won 4 pennants and 2 World Championships with them. His 1906 team set a major league record of 116 victories.

Frank Chance started out as a catcher with the Cubs and played that position for 5 seasons, until his manager, Frank Selee, argued him into becoming a first baseman. He threatened to quit baseball rather than play first base in Chicago and it took a lot of words and a raise in salary to change his mind. But once the change had been made, he became a first-rate infielder; anchor man of the great double-play combination, Tinker to Evers to Chance. He succeeded Selee as manager in the middle of the 1905 season and after that the club, under his leadership, never finished lower than third.

When he was dropped by the Cubs in 1913 and signed with

Mordecai (Three-Finger)
Brown, (left) lost most of his
index finger in a corn-chopping
machine. This accident
gave him a "natural" sinker ball.

Frank Chance, peerless
leader of the Chicago Cubs,
did not want to be
a first baseman. But his
boss insisted and
Chance became a great one.

Happy Jack Chesbro
(above) won 41 games for
the New York
Americans in 1904.

The best infield in baseball
at the turn of the
century was this gang
from the Boston Beaneaters:
Tenney, 1b, standing;
Collins, 3b, on floor;
Lowe, 2b, left;
and Long, ss, right.

the New York American League club as manager, there was a parade and a gigantic floral tribute to welcome him to the Big Town.

Frank Chance's playing career was shortened by his inability or his unwillingness to get out of the way of inside pitches. He was hit on the head many times and long suffered from severe headaches. But he was tough and unyielding and in love with baseball and stayed in the game as long as there was anyone to make room for him. After he left the big leagues, he bought the Pacific Coast League Club in Los Angeles and managed it for the seasons of 1916 and 1917. In 1923, a year before his death, he came back to the big leagues to manage the Boston Red Sox.

JOHN DWIGHT CHESBRO the big tough lad from

North Adams, Massachusetts, was nicknamed "Happy Jack" because he often wore a grin, and called "Algernon" (the current synonym for "sissy") for the same reason that a fat boy is called "Skinny." Jack was only 5 feet 9 inches tall but he was built like a small horse and he was hard as nails from his neck to his ankles.

Chesbro is the only pitcher who ever led both major leagues in won-lost percentages. In 1902, with the Pittsburgh team, he topped the National League with a record of .824. In 1904, with New York, he led the American League with a percentage of .759. That year he won 41 games for the New York team and came within one pitch of winning them a pennant. His wild pitch in the next to the last game of the season, against Boston, gave Boston the game and the championship. But without him, the New York team would never have been that close. Of his 41 victories, he won 14 in a row.

Happy Jack started playing professional ball at the age of 21, with Albany of the New York League, and moved that same season (1895) to the Springfield team of the Eastern League. He played with Roanoke and Richmond in the minors before signing in 1899 with Pittsburgh of the National League. He spent 11 seasons in the major leagues, winding up with the Boston Red Sox, in 1909.

Chesbro, whose specialty was the spitball, was one of the

last of the true iron men of the game, who were ready to pitch every day if they were asked. In 1904, in 55 games, he pitched a total of 454 innings. He struck out 239 that year and gave but 89 bases on balls. The crucial game that year, in which he made the wild pitch, he worked in because he insisted on it. He had been ordered to stay in New York when the team went to Boston to "win the pennant." He made the trip despite orders and talked Manager Clark Griffith into starting him in the first game there. Knocked out of the box in that game, he returned to New York with the team and started again 2 days later, his third start in a row. He was determined to win number 42 and to capture the pennant too.

Happy Jack actually got two of the six hits his team made that day, but, with two out and the winning run on third base in the ninth inning, one of his spitballs took off and sailed far over the catcher's head. Jack's friends always argued it was not a wild pitch at all. But others who saw it agreed the catcher could not have reached it with a ladder.

FREDERICK CLIFFORD CLARKE was one of the

greatest player-managers who ever performed. For 16 seasons he led the Pittsburgh team and for all but 4 of those seasons he was a regular in the outfield, batting over .300 in 8 of them.

He began his managerial career early, with Louisville in the National League, in 1897, when he was 24 years old; and that year, to celebrate his appointment, he hit for an average of .406, his best in the majors. He moved to Pittsburgh in 1900, along with Barney Dreyfuss, the Louisville owner, and most of the best players on the Louisville roster. Clarke stayed with Pittsburgh for the rest of his career. In 1925, he returned to Pittsburgh as a coach and the next year became a vice-president of the club.

Clarke, an Iowa farm boy, started playing baseball when he was selling newspapers in Des Moines and became a star in the Newsboys' League there. He began as a professional in the Nebraska State League, played half a season with St. Joseph in the fast Western Association and then moved to the Southern League, where he played with Montgomery and Savannah, before signing with Louisville, in the majors. He

Jack Chesbro (above) posing about 1909.
Jimmy Collins (right) in 1901 managed Boston A. L.
McGraw (right) greets Mgr. Fred Clarke of Pittsburgh (below).

Horner
Photo

made his major league debut on June 30, 1894, when he was not yet 22 years old. Before he ended his active career he had made 2703 hits in 2204 games. His lifetime average is .315.

As a manager of Pittsburgh, Clarke won 4 pennants and 1 World Championship and led his team in the first World Series ever played: the Boston-Pittsburgh Series in 1903.

JAMES JOSEPH COLLINS is well remembered today when a third baseman dashes toward the plate to make a barehanded scoop and throw of a bunt, for he made that play famous. He was not perhaps the first third baseman to handle a bunted ball this way, but he made a specialty of it and taught all those who followed him that it was the only way to beat the runner.

Jimmy, born in Buffalo, made his big-league start and made his reputation in Boston, where he played for both the National and American League teams.

Never a top slugger, Jimmy was still a timely hitter and in 1897, with the Boston Beaneaters, he posted a batting average of .346, his lifetime high. His lifetime average was .294. He was at his best, however, as an infield strategist. In his day, combination plays in the infield were not common and when he and Fred Tenney, Boston's first baseman, teamed up to nail unwary baserunners who wandered from the bag, the crowds used to scream in excitement.

Jimmy started playing professional ball in his home town, when he was 20. He played 2 seasons with Buffalo, then signed with the Beaneaters, who soon sent him on "loan" to Louisville. Next season he was back in Boston to stay for a dozen years. Under his leadership, the Boston Puritans of the American League won 2 pennants, in 1903 and 1904. They played (and won) only 1 World Series, however, for the New York Giants refused to play the representatives of the "bush league" in 1904.

THOMAS HENRY CONNOLLY British-born, never played baseball in his life. He started out as an umpire and finished his career as one. In the early 1890's, Tim Hurst, the National League umpire, who used to borrow a mask to umpire a game, discovered Tom Connolly umpiring for a Y.M.C.A. club in Natick, Massachusetts. He liked Tom's work so well he recommended him to the pros. Tom put in 4 seasons umpiring in the New England League, worked 2 seasons in the National League, and in 1901 joined the umpiring staff of the new American League. He stayed there 28 years, then in 1931 was made Umpire-in-Chief. Tom was a fair and fearless man who faced down the toughest of them, including John McGraw. In Tom's first year in the American League he thumbed ten players out of the game and made his order stick.

EDWARD JAMES DELAHANTY of the five Delahanty brothers who played big-league baseball, was the oldest, the biggest, and the best. Big Ed was one of baseball's first great sluggers. Born in Cleveland, Ohio, just after the Civil War was over, he never saw the cork-centered ball, nor had a chance to hit when pitchers were forbidden to use foreign substances to roughen or darken the ball. But he struck some mighty blows just the same.

One day he broke a third baseman's ankle with a daisy-cutter that barely skimmed the dirt. Another time he laid into a well-worn ball so hard he broke it in two. And no other player in the major leagues has ever led both leagues in hitting: Big Ed led the National League in 1899; the American League, in 1902. Twice in his major league career he made 6 hits in 6 times at bat.

Playing second, first, and in the outfield, Ed began with the Mansfield team of the Ohio State league when he was 19 years old. Later, he joined the Philadelphia Nationals. He did not really begin to murder the ball, however, until 1892, when he was back in Philadelphia. That year he hit for an average of .312, and from that day forth he never dropped below .319. In 1899, he led the National League with an average of .408. He jumped to Washington in the American League in 1902 and immediately led that league with a mark of .376.

Bid Ed's greatest day came in Chicago in 1896 when he hit 4 home runs and a single in 5 times at bat.

Umpire Tom Connolly worked
in both National and American
Leagues over 34-year span.

John Evers (right) was the
brains of the Chicago Cub infield
for eleven seasons (1903-1913).

John Evers of Troy, N. Y. weighed
only 105 pounds when he
joined the Chicago Cubs in 1902.

Big Ed Delahanty, shown here in the 1880's, with Philadelphia, was still murdering the ball when the New Century
came in. Mustaches had disappeared from baseball by then.

JOHN J. EVERS when he joined the Chicago Cubs in 1902, weighed with a wet towel around his waist, 105 pounds, not really enough to qualify him for a job on a high-school team. The Cubs had taken him as a sort of makeweight in a trade, with a pitcher named Hardy. The price was $250 and the Cubs, after they took a look at the lantern-jawed youngster, thought they had been robbed. He was a grimly determined young man, however, and they gave him a try at shortstop, where he made 8 errors in his first 4 games. That would have finished him with the Cubs had not second baseman Bobby Lowe been injured. Evers was moved into that slot and stayed there. He'd have torn anyone apart who had tried to move him out.

Scrap, wit, determination, and speed kept John Evers in the big leagues. Like McGraw, Hughey Jennings, and Willie Keeler, he was forever scheming out ways to get an extra base or an extra run, or to seize any advantage over an opponent. He was no heavy hitter, yet he managed to get on base an inordinate number of times and twice actually hit over .300. With Joe Tinker and Frank Chance, he became the pivot man in the most famous infield combination in the game; and he was probably the ablest fielder who ever played second base, except for Eddie Collins.

Nicknamed "the Crab," because of the manner in which he scuttled about the infield, and the testy nature he displayed in his dealings with umpires and opponents, Johnnie Evers, after winning fame with the Chicago Cubs, went on to the Braves to become a hero in Boston. Here he teamed with another tough little character named Rabbit Maranville, to needle, cajole, scheme, encourage, and beseech his team-mates into a pennant—a miracle it was called and the credit was given to Manager Stallings. But Johnnie Evers, who was playing baseball in his mind through every waking hour, was the real spark plug.

URBAN CLARENCE (RED) FABER, one of the last four spitballers who were allowed to employ their specialty after this delivery had been outlawed, was also perhaps the only baseball player of Luxemburg ancestry. Born in Iowa in 1888, big Red spent his entire big-league career with one team—the Chicago White Sox.

Red was a tireless pitcher who toiled long and hard for a team that seldom finished in the first division. Yet he won more than 20 games in 4 seasons and in 1917, when his club did get into the World Series, he won three Series games. His best year came early in his career. In 1915, when he was 26 years old, he worked in 50 games for the White Sox and won 24 of them, while losing 13. He struck out 182 batters that year, the best he ever did in that department.

Red Faber was a switch-hitter, but he threw with his right hand. He stayed in the big leagues with the White Sox for 20 seasons and pitched over 4000 innings of baseball. A bad arm kept Red out of the 1919 World Series, in which several of his teammates were besmirched by charges of throwing games. But Red came back in the 1920's stronger than before, to win 21 games or more three years in a row. In 1922, with 21 victories, he posted his second-highest strike-out total: 148. Red was not a fireball pitcher nor a strike-out king. He relied heavily on his dipsy-doodling spitball to keep the batters rolling the ball to the infielders.

Faber actually did pitch for another major-league team, but his work was unofficial. Immediately after he had been purchased by the White Sox, Red was offered on loan to the New York Giants and went on a world tour with them. He beat his own club 4 times on the trip. Faber started his pitching career with St. Joseph's College in Dubuque, Iowa, and entered professional baseball with Dubuque in the Three-Eye League. While with Dubuque he pitched the first perfect game in minor-league history, beating Davenport 3 to 0 without letting a man reach first.

Red Faber, one of the last of the spitballers.

CLARK CALVIN GRIFFITH the Old Fox of major league baseball, was a very young fox when he started playing organized ball in Bloomington, Illinois. He was not yet 19 when he pitched 14 games for Bloomington and won 10 of them. He made his final active appearance 26 years later, as a pitcher for Washington in the American League. He stayed in organized baseball all his life, as manager and finally president of the Washington Senators.

As a major league manager, Clark Griffith never had a pennant winner, although his Senators won three pennants after he became president. His foxiness showed itself chiefly in his shrewd dealing in ballplayers. He combined veterans and youngsters to turn a last-place team into a pennant contender. When he started in Washington, Griffith seemed like a miracle man. He took over a ball club that had never placed higher than sixth and put them in second place 2 years in a row. Griffith was also a showman and more than once hired a ballplayer for his ability as a clown. Griffith was one of the original organizers of the American League and he put together the first New York team in that league, through wily "raiding" of the National League rosters. This skill at finding players (or managers) when he needed them earned him his nickname and remained his stock in trade.

Clark Griffith was pitching for the Cubs in 1900. In 1901 he jumped to the White Sox.

HUGHEY AMBROSE JENNINGS was one of the most famous graduates of the old Baltimore Orioles, in the days when they were the toughest team in the National League. Hughey was a little fellow, only 5 feet 8, but he was tough and full of fight. When he was playing shortstop for Baltimore he had a private motto: "Hit or get hit." If he could not get hold of a good pitch, he did not hesitate to get his body in the way of the ball, so he could get first base for free. His left side, in those days, was almost one wide bruise from the pitched balls that had hit him there.

Hughey's strategic skill and his burning desire to win earned him more fame than his bat did, but he did post 5 good over-.300 averages in 1894 and the seasons immediately following, when the pitching distance had been increased to 60 feet 6 inches. He was a one-man show on the coaching lines, especially when managing the Detroit Tigers, from 1907 to 1920. His battle cry of "Eeee-yah!" was famous all around the circuit and fans used to join him sometimes in this scream of triumph. He would wave both arms, with his fists tightly clenched, and kick one foot in the air when he emitted this cry, which eventually became his nickname.

When he began to slow down as a player he turned to managing, in the minor leagues first (when Baltimore had

Hughey Jennings in his famous pose, yelling "Eeee-yah!"

lost its major league franchise) and then in Detroit, where he earned even greater fame as a manager than he had known as a player.

A crafty batsman who, like all the Orioles, was a skillful bunter, Hughey had a lifetime major league batting average of .314. He 4 times led all National League shortstops in fielding percentage. In his 3 years as a major league manager (1907-9) he won 3 American League pennants for Detroit.

BYRON BANCROFT JOHNSON is honored as the
man who founded the American League and became its first president. But Ban did far more than that. It was he who first insisted that the flagrant bullying of umpires must cease and that umpires hired by the league be backed up in their decisions even though an entire ball club, including the owner, should be arrayed against them.

Johnson never played professional baseball, but he was a college catcher. After graduation he became a reporter for the Cincinnati Commercial-Gazette and gave as much time to writing about baseball as his employers would allow. When Charles Comiskey left his job as manager of the Chicago National League team to manage the Reds in 1892, Johnson joined him and a few other in planning the Western Association—a minor league that hoped for major status—with teams in Detroit, Grand Rapids, Indianapolis, Kansas City, Milwaukee, Minneapolis, Toledo, and Sioux City. In 1899, by a mere change of name, this grouping became the American League.

Johnson was a strong president but not all his edicts won immediate acceptance. He tried for instance to put an end to "organized rooting" on the part of spectators, who had begun to form in groups to make loud noises in concert, like college boys at a football game. The fans, however, simply would not obey and eventually rhythmic clapping, cheering, booing, and even cries of "Take him out!" became a part of baseball tradition.

On the field, however, thanks to Ban Johnson, the baseball umpire now controls the game, for he knows that his orders cannot be countermanded by manager or club owner.

Bancroft Johnson, a former sports writer,
founded a new major league in 1901.

WILLIAM J. KLEM a tough little man who never
played big-league baseball, is perhaps the most famous
umpire who ever lived. Known as "the Old Arbitrator," Klem
almost by himself raised the standard of umpiring in the
National League. He was cool, determined, and convinced
that he was right. He permitted no baseball player to take
liberties with him and he devoted himself to his job with a
religious fervor. Indeed, just before his retirement, he an-
nounced at a dinner given in his honor: "Baseball is not a
game with me—it's a religion!"

Bill Klem, who wound up his career as supervisor of um-

Bill Klem, "the Old Arbitrator,"
would never admit he had called a
play wrong in his life.
No player dared disagree.

Umpires, in the old days,
required a megaphone man to
announce the batteries.
Bill Klem holds mask;
Connolly, next to megaphone.

pires in the National League, always maintained control of the baseball game he was umpiring. Players who approached him to argue a decision were warned: "Don't cross the Rio Grande!" The "Rio Grande" was a line drawn in the dirt by the toe of Bill Klem's shoe. If the player stepped across it, he was out of the game, and he knew it.

Bill Klem taught umpires to stay on top of the plays, so that their decisions could be made on the basis of a close view of what had happened. He invented the behind-the-plate stance that all umpires use today.

CHRISTOPHER MATHEWSON when he first
played baseball for pay, was a cross-handed batter, strong, awkward, extremely willing, and only 14 years old.

His most famous pitch was named the "fadeaway" and it is compared to today's screwball—a reverse curve. But he also had a "dry spitter" that must have been a form of knuckle ball. He was a brainy pitcher, and a strong one who never seemed to tire. In 3 successive seasons with the New York Giants (1903-5) he won 30 games or more. And in the World Series of 1905, he won 3 games for the Giants— all shutouts. In 16 full seasons with the Giants he won 20 games or better 13 times. His high mark was 1908, when out of 56 games he pitched, he won 37 and lost 11, setting the "modern" record for wins in the National League. He also set the modern league record for strikeouts, with 267 in 1903. He pitched 2 no-hit games: one against St. Louis in 1901 and one against Chicago in 1905.

A master of control and an easy worker, Mathewson could go inning after inning without giving up a base on balls. Between June 19 and July 18, 1913, he pitched 68 innings in a row without allowing a walk—the record. In 1916, when his left arm (which was not his pitching arm) began to pain him, he went to Cincinnati to become manager there. He pitched only 1 game for Cincinnati and won that 10-8. He left this job to enter the army in World War I, was gassed in the trenches, and came back to act for a time as coach with the Giants. Soon afterward he was made president of the Boston Braves and held this position until his untimely death in 1925.

Gentle Christy Mathewson and tough John McGraw (right), his manager, with the N. Y. Giants about 1903.

CORNELIUS McGILLICUDDY was known all his

life as Connie Mack, for that was the way his neighbors in East Brookfield, Massachusetts, shortened his name so they could pronounce it. Connie, like most young males in East Brookfield, started to work in the local shoe factory. In his spare time he played baseball and soon played it well enough to make a living at it. He kept on making his living at the game, with his hard hands, his quick wit, and his shrewd brain, until he was 88 years old.

Called "Slats" as a boy, Connie early in his career teamed with another skinny lad, named Frank Gilmore, to become the Bones Battery—Mack catching and Gilmore pitching. Together they formed the best combination in the Connecticut State League. Connie was not the greatest catcher nor the heaviest batter of his day. But he owned the sharpest tongue and the quickest wit, and he talked many an able batter out of a base hit. In the National League, which he and Gilmore entered (with the Washington Statesmen) in 1886, Mack soon won fame as "the talking catcher," and fans used to gather just to enjoy the sound of his comically high-pitched voice.

Connie Mack first became a manager with Buffalo in the Players' League during the Brotherhood Strike but wound up with the Pittsburgh Nationals when the strike was over. A broken ankle received when he blocked the plate against Herman Long of Boston slowed Connie down, so he began to see the end of his playing career, and he was quick to accept an offer to manage the Pittsburgh team in 1894. He remained an active manager for another 55 years—with Milwaukee of the Western League and then with Philadelphia of the new American League, where he also became the owner of the club.

Connie Mack is best remembered now for the manner in which he used to run his team from the bench. Always dressed in hard collar, hard straw hat, and business suit, Connie waved his fielders into position with his folded score card— placing them, he once explained, with no false modesty, "so the fly balls would drop in their hands."

Connie won 9 pennants with his Philadelphia Athletics—

At left, Connie Mack, 90, and
Cy Young, 86, meet at Cooperstown,
N. Y. in 1952 to participate
in ceremonies at National
Baseball Hall of Fame.

Above, veteran Connie Mack,
50, talks with the
young president of the
Connecticut State League,
W. J. Tracey, in 1912.

In 1905, manager Connie Mack won his first American League pennant with this club. Chief Bender (whom Connie always called Albert) is at his right shoulder. Kneeling in front of Bender, Rube Waddell.

although in its earliest days his team was hard put to pay the groundskeeper—and his teams took 5 World Championships. Even when Connie was nearing 90, his team was sometimes in the thick of the race and Connie still found time to appraise young ballplayers and to write long letters, in a steady, legible hand, about how great some rookie catcher might be "in years to come."

Iron Man McGinnity firing "Old Sal," his underhand pitch.

JOSEPH JEROME McGINNITY became famous as the Iron Man in 1903 when he pitched 5 double-headers for the New York Giants, winning 3 of them (in the same month) and dividing the other 2. He was a tireless pitcher. Using a half-sidearm, half-underhand pitch he called "Old Sal," he seldom struck a man out, but the pop-ups were numerous. Often he could retire the side on 5 or 6 pitched balls.

Joe was 28 years old when he finally landed in the big leagues, with Baltimore of the National League. He won 27 games his first year, then moved to Brooklyn (when Baltimore was dropped from the league) and won 27 more. In his first 6 days on the Brooklyn team he pitched and won 5 ball games but his fame did not spread across the nation until he began to win double-headers for the Giants.

He won only 9 games in his first year with New York, perhaps because he was busy playing second base and the outfield as well as pitching. But in 1903, he won 31 and in 1904, when the Giants won the pennant, Iron Man McGinnity won 35. In his 11 years in the majors he never had a losing season.

After he was through in the majors, Iron Man McGinnity earned his title all over again by pitching for 17 more seasons in the minor leagues, winning a total of 204 games there. In his final season, with Dubuque, a team he was managing, at the age of 54 Joe won 6 out of 12 games. He "retired" then to go back to the big leagues as a coach.

JOHN JOSEPH McGRAW is famed today because of his accomplishments as leader of the New York Giants, whom he managed for 31 years, and with whom he won 10 pennants and 3 Worlds Championships. But before he came to New York, he was known all through the baseball world as the tough little third baseman of the Baltimore Orioles, a scrappy, hard-hitting, quick-thinking and fast-moving little Irishman with a thin bony face and prominent ears, who feared no man and apparently felt all umpires were his mortal enemies. A forceful, even overbearing man, he had almost as many enemies as he had friends; but most of the men who played for him were fiercely loyal to him and some of them, becoming managers themselves, spread the McGraw gospel throughout baseball, imitating his pet plays, his training methods, his strategy, so that his impress on baseball was as great as that of any man who ever played the game.

As a player, McGraw shone brightest in Baltimore where he and Willie Keeler perfected the bunt and especially the foul bunt, which they used to wear pitchers down. But little John could hit the ball hard and in 1895 attained a batting average of .374. That year he stole 69 bases and in 1898 he stole 73. His lifetime batting average was .334. It was in Baltimore that McGraw learned the baseball strategy that was to make

John McGraw (left), near
the end of his career as
Giants' manager.

Wilbert Robinson (above),
led the Brooklyn Dodgers to a
pennant in 1920.

him one of the two or three great managers of all time. Some he learned from Ned Hanlon, his manager there, and the rest he learned from his teammates, as they sat up late nights to devise tricks, tactics, signals, and stunts to win the ball game next day. Winning was McGraw's religion when he was on the baseball diamond, and close teamwork, which meant loyalty and readiness to give all for the team, was the chief article of his faith.

Starting as a Sunday semi-pro at the age of 17, McGraw worked quickly up to organized baseball. He was a pitcher when he started but was soon switched to shortstop and finally to third base. He entered organized ball with Olean (New York) of the New York-Pennsylvania League, and went from there to Cedar Rapids, in the Illinois-Iowa League. In 1891, before the season was over, he quit Cedar Rapids to take a job with Baltimore in the American Association and landed in the National League when the League expanded to 12 clubs and added the Baltimore franchise.

He managed Baltimore in 1899, was sent to St. Louis next year to become manager there, and then jumped to the Baltimore team in the American League in 1901. A season and a half with Ban Johnson, who did not approve of abusing umpires, was enough for McGraw and he jumped back into the National League to take over the New York team and to turn it within a few seasons from a seventh-place club to a pennant winner.

When he retired in 1932, his fame was world-wide. Many baseball men who learned their strategy from him still mention his name with reverence.

WILBERT ROBINSON spent so many years (1914-1931) as nonplaying manager of the Brooklyn Dodgers, who were often called the Robins in his honor, that many fans forgot that he had ever been a ballplayer himself. Yet he had 17 seasons in the majors, as a catcher with an occasional stint at first base. One season at Baltimore (1896) he batted .354. And on June 10, 1892, he made 7 hits (6 singles and a double) in 7 times at bat.

Robbie was one of the most aggressive and vocal members

of the scrappy Baltimore Orioles, who started in the American Association and wound up in the National League. To stay on that team, a ballplayer, besides being tough and aggressive, had to be smart and able to extemporize on the field of play. These skills helped make Robbie into a successful manager. But before he took over in Brooklyn, Robbie managed the Baltimore club in the American League, stayed with them when they landed in the Eastern (minor) League, and worked three seasons as coach with John McGraw and the New York Giants.

Robinson won only 2 pennants with the Brooklyn Dodgers (1916 and 1920). But his team was always in contention and was always unpredictable. There was always excitement at the Brooklyn ball park and the club prospered with Robbie at the helm.

Robbie's 1916 champions, like so many Brooklyn clubs, seemed to be made up of players nobody else wanted. But Robbie urged and schemed and maneuvered them into the flag, beating out the other 3 eastern clubs in the league by a close margin.

JOSEPH BERT TINKER
head man in the Tinker-to-Evers-to-Chance double-play combination, spent all his major league career in Chicago.

Never a strong man at the plate, Joe topped .300 only when he was in Cincinnati. His great fame was earned by his fielding, and by his unerring teamwork in making the Cubs' infield impregnable through the early 1900's. Joe was not a tall man, only 5 feet 9, but he was solidly built and fleet of foot. In 1908, when the Cubs won the pennant, Joe topped all the shortstops in fielding percentage and in assists. In the World Series that year he handled 27 chances without an error.

He and Johnny Evers, the second baseman, played together like parts of a machine, using private and silent signals to indicate who was to cover second base on the coming play. In this way they were often able to smother hit-and-run plays by closing the expected "hole" in the infield. Yet for years

Denton True Young was called "Cy."
He said it was short for "Cyclone."

The start of a famous double play:
Tinker, to Evers, to Chance. Tinker
has just tossed ball to Evers, in
pivot. Evers drags his foot across
the base to make the first out and
prepares to throw over to Chance.

Rube Waddell liked to be called Eddie.

he and Evers did not speak to each other off the field.

Born in Kansas, Joe Tinker played his first professional baseball in Coffeyville, Kansas, joined the Denver club of the Western League when he was 19 years old, but finished that first season with the Great Falls-Helena team of the Montana State League. He advanced to Portland of the Pacific North-West League next season and led the league's shortstops in fielding percentage, in putouts and assists—and in errors too. He was promptly brought up to Chicago. He did not really come into his own there until Frank Chance was made manager. Then he and Evers and Chance took over the defensive strategy and made the Cubs nearly unbeatable for the next five years.

GEORGE EDWARD WADDELL was "Eddie" to

his friends and would punch a stranger in the nose who called him "Rube" to his face. But finally he grew to like the name and applied it to himself when he urged fans in St. Louis (in signs he painted on the sidewalk) to "come out and see Rube fan 'em out!" That was toward the very end of his career, after he had earned national fame as a great pitcher and a great eccentric in Philadelphia and in several minor league cities.

In the big leagues, the only man with patience enough to handle Rube, who loved to take days off for fishing, or for riding fire engines, or for playing marbles with kids, was Connie Mack, for whom he did his best big-league pitching in Milwaukee and Philadelphia. Playing for Connie Mack with Milwaukee in the American League, Rube struck out an average of 5 men a game. When he settled down (more or less) in Philadelphia with Connie, he reveled in the new fame that was his and responded with some extraordinary pitching. In his first year, 1902, with Philadelphia he won 23 games and struck out 210, leading the league in that department as he was to lead it five more times.

In 1908, when Waddell would no longer respond to discipline, Connie had to trade his big Rube to St. Louis, where he came back to trim the Athletics with 16 strikeouts in one game—a record that stood for years. Although Rube won 19 games in each of his first 2 seasons in St. Louis, he never again attained the heights he reached with Philadelphia, where he won 27 games in 1905, while losing but 10.

DENTON TRUE YOUNG called Cy (for Cyclone) was the pitching marvel of all time, reliable, indestructible, and frequently unhittable. He pitched more games than any other pitcher in baseball (906), pitched for more years in the majors than anyone else (23), and won more games than any pitcher before or since (511). He also established a record for consecutive hitless innings (23). That mark was set in 1904, when Cy was 37 years old. That same year he pitched a "perfect" game (allowing not a single batter to reach base) for Boston against Philadelphia. He had previously pitched a no-hitter, in 1897, for Cleveland against Cincinnati in the National League; and in 1908, when he was 41, he threw another no-hitter for the Boston American League club against the New York Highlanders. In the minor leagues when he was pitching for Canton against McKeesport (Tri-State League) in 1890, he threw a no-hit game too and struck out 18 batters.

In 1890, he joined the Cleveland club of the National League. He pitched 8 full seasons for Cleveland, never winning fewer than 21 games and one season winning 36.

After 2 years in St. Louis (26-15, 19-18), he signed with Boston, in the new American League. He pitched there for 8 seasons, winning 33 games his very first year. In 1903, he won 2 games for Boston in the first World Series ever played between the National and American Leagues. In 1908, he was sold to Cleveland, and in 1911, at the age of 44, he jumped the league fence still another time, to sign with the Boston Braves. He won 4 games for them and lost 5 before calling it a career. His pitching arm was still strong enough, he insisted, but he could not field his position as fast as he used to and the opposition was wearing him down with bunts.

When Cy was 80 years old, actively farming in Newcomerstown, Ohio, he wrote to an inquirer concerning the speed of two fast-ball contemporaries, Amos Rusie and Walter Johnson. "Do not believe," he wrote, "that either one was quite up to me in speed."

ALTHOUGH THE SPEEDY CORK-CENTERED BALL WAS INTRODUCED IN 1911, THE GAME STRATEGY WAS STILL BASED ON THE DEAD BALL. DOMINATING THE ERA WERE THE PITCHERS WHO DISCOVERED HOW TO HOLD BASE-RUNNERS, WHICH CUT BASE-STEALING IN HALF. DESPITE THESE ADVANCEMENTS, STEALING, BUNTING AND SCHEMING RE-MAINED OF GREAT IMPORTANCE IN THE DEVELOPMENT OF THE GAME.

DEAD BALL

John Franklin Baker became "Home Run" Baker in 1911 when he hit two home runs in the same World Series. But his real strong point was his sturdy and agile work with the glove. He was one of the best-fielding 3rd basemen in the game.

JOHN FRANKLIN BAKER actually hit fewer home

runs in his major league career (93) than Babe Ruth hit in two successive years (114 in 1927-28). But Frank was hitting them when the ball was "dead" and home runs were a rarity. He led the American League in home runs 4 years in a row, with 9 in 1911, 10 in 1912, 12 in 1913, and 8 in 1914. But he got his nickname "Home Run" by winning 2 World Series games with home runs: in 1911 and in 1913. And in 1911 he hit 2 home runs in the same World Series.

Frank was a standout third baseman. As a hitter he had a lifetime major league mark of .308 and the highest average he achieved was .347 in 1912. As a fielder he led his league in putouts in 7 seasons and in 1917 and 1918, when he was with the New York Americans, he led all American League third basemen in fielding percentage. In 1914, in 4 successive games, Frank accepted 25 chances at third base without an error, making 10 putouts and 15 assists.

A powerful right-handed farm boy who batted left-handed, Frank was the left-hand corner of Connie Mack's $100,000 infield—supposed to be the best fielding crew ever put together. With Stuffy McInnis, Eddie Collins, and Jack Barry, Frank Baker formed a Maginot Line against enemy hitters, ranging far out on the grass or in front of the infield position to handle more chances than any rival third baseman in the league.

CHARLES ALBERT BENDER like all Indians in

baseball, was known as "Chief." His own chief, Connie Mack of the Philadelphia Athletics, always addressed him as Albert, however, and this seemed more fitting for this quiet, easy-going young man who was one-quarter Chippewa Indian. (His father was Dutch and his mother half-Chippewa.)

Chief Bender learned his baseball at the Carlisle Indian School in Carlisle, Pennsylvania, and he entered professional baseball with the Athletics the year after he graduated from Carlisle.

Bender was only 19 when he joined the Athletics. He was a poised young man all the same and he stepped into stardom without a flutter. In his first season, 1903, Chief Bender won 17 of the 34 games he worked in. Four of his first 5 seasons were winning seasons and his eighth season with Connie Mack was his best. That was 1910, when he won 23 games and led the league in won-lost percentage.

Bender, who had the steadiest nerves in the game, also had remarkable eyesight—as sharp as that of the greatest hitters.

Chief Bender pitched in 5 World Series for Connie Mack, worked in 10 games and won 6 of them. He led the American League in won-lost percentage three times while he was with the Athletics: in 1910, 1911, and 1914. He played most of his remaining years in the minors.

MAX GEORGE CAREY who started out in life
named Maximilian Carnarius, was never a great slugger; but he holds an impressive collection of major league records, most of them because of his speed. He was fast on the bases and fast getting on base. He was swift in the outfield and swift crossing the plate. Carey holds the modern National League lifetime record for total stolen bases: 738. He led his league in stolen bases ten times between 1913 and 1925. In 1916 he stole 63 bases.

Max was adept at reading a pitcher's movements so as to get a quick start. He was not a wild man on the bases like Cobb and a few others, but once he took off for the next base, he usually made it. In 1922, he attempted 53 steals and was successful 51 times.

In the outfield, Carey accepted more chances than any other National League outfielder before him: 6702. Six times he made more than 400 putouts in a season in the outfield; and he established a league record by playing more games in the outfield than anyone else: 2421. In 9 seasons he led all National League outfielders in putouts.

Born in Terre Haute, Indiana, Carey set out to study for the ministry at Concordia College, in St. Louis. But they had a baseball team there and young Max became a pitcher, playing shortstop in between whiles. With his studies completed, Carey joined the South Bend team, and was placed in left field. When he moved up to Pittsburgh (after stealing 86 bases

Chief Bender pitched in
five World Series,
won six Series games.

Home Run Baker (left),
favored old style
of turned-up collar.

Max Carey, Pittsburgh
speedster, studied for
the ministry.

in 96 games) young Carey still worked out at short from time to time. But the outfield was where he stayed—and it was the outfield rather than the ministry that proved to be his calling.

Max was a switch hitter, although he was a natural right-hander. He batted lead-off for Pittsburgh and one season (1922) scored 120 runs. In 1925, he made his top mark as a batter: .343.

TYRUS RAYMOND COBB like Babe Ruth, deserves a Hall of Fame all by himself, he stands so far ahead of all his contemporaries in nearly every department of the game. Even Babe Ruth, with no effort to be modest, solemnly averred that Ty Cobb was the greatest ballplayer who ever lived, and Babe pitched against him when Babe himself was at his best on the mound.

Ty Cobb was not a "natural" athlete in the sense that any of his accomplishments came without trying. He owed his eminence to endless practice and indomitable determination. He just would not take second place to anyone, regardless of his natural skills; and if he failed in some effort on the diamond he would practice until he succeeded. Cobb broke into baseball in an age when just staying on the team required brute determination. When he was a rookie, his teammates broke his bats, bumped him aside in batting practice, cut holes in his shoes, and even locked him out of his hotel room. He had to fight for his place on the team and he had to fight to win ball games.

Batting was his special skill. No one in the American League ever earned a higher batting average than he did and only one man (George Sisler) equaled his high mark of .420, which Cobb made in 1911. But hitting safely was not just a matter of meeting the ball with the bat. It required careful placing of the ball sometimes, a fast start, and often a determined slide. Although he threw right-handed Cobb batted left-handed because it put him closer to first. He held his hands well apart on the bat so he could adjust to the pitch and to the strategic situation. If the infielders played him close, he might slap the ball past them. If they played him deep, he would dump the ball in front of them and beat the throw. If a

When Ty Cobb
came to Detroit
he had to
fight for his
turn in batting
practice.

Ty Cobb sometimes
played first base. Here
he wears a first-baseman's
glove and carries
an outfielder's.

Cobb roars into
base (above) while fielder
leaps for his life.

pitch was too far outside, and the situation required a hit, he might throw his bat at the ball and still hit it safely.

On the baselines he was a terror. He kept his spikes sharp, not merely to frighten or slash the opposing basemen (as some people said) but because sharp spikes meant better footing and a quicker start. He studied pitchers until he knew just when he could get the jump on a pitch. He slid into a base fearlessly and sometimes deliberately kicked a ball out of a waiting glove, or knocked a baseman loose from it. He allowed no one the right to stand between him and the base he wanted.

As a batter, he led the American League 12 times; and he led the league six times in stolen bases. He holds the American League record in games played, times at bat, total runs scored, stolen bases, total hits, and total three-base hits (the type of hit that best indicates speed on the basepaths and the willingness to try for that extra base). In 1922, when he had been in the big leagues 17 years, he four times made 5 hits in one game—a modern record. On May 5, 1925, he made 6 hits in 6 times at bat. In 1915, he made the league record for stolen bases: 96. His lifetime batting average, the highest of any Hall-of-Famer, was .367.

As a manager, Cobb was most successful in teaching his batting tricks to others. Harry Heilmann, the great right-handed batter, credited Cobb with making a batting champion out of him.

Cobb, after a season in the bushes, spent 22 seasons with the Detroit Tigers, then ended his career, at the age of 41, by hitting .323 in 95 games with the Philadelphia Athletics. He remained close to the game all his life and gave frequent advice on player deals to George Weiss, the great builder of the New York Yankees and Cobb's lifelong friend.

An outfielder all through his career, Cobb usually played first base in exhibition games, once played second base for Detroit, and in 1925, when he was managing Detroit, actually pitched a game (to no decision).

EDWARD TROWBRIDGE COLLINS second
baseman in Connie Mack's famous $100,000 infield, shares

with Bobby Wallace a record for consecutive years as an active player in the major leagues: 25. He started playing professional baseball when he was still attending Columbia University, and he played his first game with the Philadelphia Athletics when he had just turned 19. He went to bat only 15 times that season (1906) and got but 3 hits. In 1907, he played part of the year in Philadelphia and then played 4 games with Newark, in the Eastern League. In 1908, he was back with Connie Mack's Athletics to stay until 1914, when he was sold to the Chicago White Sox. After 12 seasons there, he returned to the Athletics to finish his active career.

Eddie Collins is still considered by many authorities the best defensive second baseman the game ever saw. But he was a great hitter and runner too. He had a lifetime average of .333 with a high mark (in 1920) of .369. In 1910 and in 1919 he led the league in stolen bases and he still holds the modern record of 6 bases stolen in 1 game. He did this twice in the same year: September 11 and 22, 1912.

Another baseball art that Collins was a master of was stealing signs and "reading" pitchers. He made a full-time study of the pitchers he faced, searching for the telltale movements that would foretell the curve, or the fast ball, or the pitch-out — or the pick-off throw. Because of this ability to decipher the opponents, Collins was an expert on the hit-and-run play, on the drag bunt (he batted left-handed), and on the squeeze. His 509 sacrifice hits is a record. He is also one of the few players ever to make 3000 base hits in the major leagues.

His ability to remember the idiosyncrasies of opposing players served Collins well in the field too. He never seemed to make any diving stops or wild dashes, yet he was always on the spot when the ball came along and could receive and get rid of the ball in the pivot of a double play faster than any man of his day. He himself had only one major idiosyncrasy: a habit of sticking a wad of chewing gum on the button of his cap and popping it into his mouth if the pitcher got 2 strikes on him. They very seldom got the third.

SAMUEL EARL CRAWFORD called Wahoo Sam

because he was born in Wahoo, Nebraska, made more three-

Harry Heilmann used Cobb style at bat.
Eddie Collins, right, played 25 years.
Sam Crawford came from Wahoo, Neb.

base hits in his big-league career than any other man who ever played. In his 4 years in the National League, Sam hit 62, and in his 15 years in the American League he hit 250.

A tall, solid young man, with oversize hands and feet, Sam Crawford gave up a barbering career and made the big leagues almost as soon as he tried. Sam's greatest fame came to him in Detroit, where he landed in 1903 after a peace settlement between the National League and the American League separated him from Cincinnati and awarded him to Detroit. (He had signed contracts with both.) Sam, who played left field and batted left-handed, immediately began to slash his long long hits to right and right-center, where they had plenty of room to roll.

Sam Crawford, along with Ty Cobb and Bobby Veach, made up Detroit's dream outfield in the pre-Babe Ruth era. All were fast, all three hit solidly, all stole bases well, and they played together as if they operated on the same strings. But Sam was finished in the big leagues before his partners wore out, for he had started a good deal sooner. After 1917, he found room for himself in the Pacific Coast League, where, at the age of 41, he was still pounding the ball for an average of .318.

ELMER HARRISON FLICK is remembered chiefly
because he led the American League 1 season (1905) with the lowest average that ever took the championship: .306. Yet he often hit for a far higher average than that. In 1900, with the Philadelphia Nationals, he hit .378. And in the minor leagues, with Dayton, he had hit .386 in 1897. He was a small solid man who, like Ty Cobb, hit from the left-handers' side of the plate, even though he threw right-handed. Like all hitters who are fast afoot, he specialized in 3-baggers, leading the league in triples for 3 successive years (1905-6-7).

In 1906 the Detroit Tigers, annoyed by the quarrelsome manners of their rookie outfielder, offered to trade Ty Cobb even-up for Elmer Flick. But the Cleveland management would have none of it. Flick was a bread-and-butter man for them, while Cobb seemed headed for a short career. But Flick suddenly developed ulcers, or some other severe stomach trouble, and began to fade badly. In 1908 he could play in only 9 games. He tried again in 1909, when he got into 66 games. In 1910 he played but 24 and then the Cleveland management reluctantly gave up on their dynamic little star. The next year, with Toledo of the American Association, he staged a sort of comeback, getting into 84 games and batting .326. In 1912, he played even more, but his hitting had fallen off badly and he had to face the fact that he was finished.

Elmer had started in organized baseball with Youngstown of the Interstate League, when he was just turned 20. He put in a year with Youngstown and a year with Dayton before the Philadelphia Nationals signed him in 1898. He spent 4 seasons in Philadelphia, pounding the ball with great authority, before he jumped to Cleveland in May 1902.

In the American League Flick exhibited both speed and power. He led the league in stolen bases in 1904 with 42, and he led again in 1906 with 39, tying with Anderson of Washington. He did not seem therefore like any less than a match for Cobb until 1908, when Cobb began to blaze away on the baselines and Flick, crippled by his stomach trouble (which some observers blamed on "the water at New Orleans"), began to weaken.

Flick was not nearly as big a man as Cobb. He stood 5 feet 8 and weighed only 160 pounds. But if his health had not given out there are those who say he would have lasted as long as the Georgia Peach, and have left a good many records of his own.

Elmer Flick
in 1906
was valued
more highly
than Ty Cobb.

BURLEIGH ARLAND GRIMES, the last of the legal spitballers, was a tough, aggressive player and a husky right-hander. He actually did not use the spitball as often as batters thought he did. He often bluffed so they always looked for it.

Grimes started his big-league career in 1916 with Pittsburgh, and after an unimpressive beginning he moved to the Brooklyn Dodgers in 1918 and became a star. In his first year with the Dodgers he won 19 games. He reached his top when he was with Pittsburgh in 1928, winning 25 games while losing 14. His highest percentage was reached the following year with Pittsburgh, when he won 17 and lost 7 for a percentage of .708.

Grimes won the first World Series game he ever pitched, —a game against Cleveland in 1920. He got into another World Series in 1930 when he was with St. Louis and lost the first game in that series to the Athletics, 5 to 2. He got his revenge the following year when he held the Athletics to 2 hits in the third game of the World Series and beat the man who had trimmed him twice previously—Lefty Bob Grove. He also won the seventh game in that series, beating Earnshaw 4 to 2. Burleigh was traded to Chicago then and appeared in the 1932 World Series against the Yankees. In 1934, he ended his career and in 1937 returned to the majors to manage the Dodgers for two years.

HARRY EDWIN HEILMANN was a good hitter when he came up to the Detroit Tigers from Portland of the Northwestern League in 1914, but he did not become a great hitter until after he had put in a season with San Francisco in the Coast League and had played 4 more seasons with Detroit. Then suddenly he began to pound out hits at the rate of almost 2 in every 5 times at bat. The difference, he said, was that Ty Cobb, his teammate at Detroit, became manager of the team and decided to show the young man how to get base hits. Before Cobb took over, Harry's best season batting average had been .320. The first year under Ty's direction (1921) Harry hit .394 and led the American League. In 1923, he led again with .403. In 1925, he led

A determined competitor, Burleigh Grimes'
grim concentration intimidated many batters.

with .393, and in 1927, he came in first again with .398.
Harry played first base, outfield, and a few games at second.
He never batted below .300 after 1919.

What Cobb did, Heilmann said, was to teach him to put
a little more weight on his front foot, to keep his arms away
from his body and his elbows high — routine advice to hitters
nowadays. But Cobb also taught big Harry (he was a 6-feet-1,
200-pound right-hander) to make a study of catchers, who
often called for the same pitch in certain circumstances, and
to learn what to expect. Cobb taught him to imitate Cobb's
stance — crouching so as to shorten the strike zone, keeping
his feet together, gripping the bat with his hands a few inches
apart. Heilmann learned quickly and developed in one season
into one of the greatest hitters in the game.

MILLER JAMES HUGGINS was a lead-off batter

and an alert fielder who batted over .300 in a full season once in 1912, with the St. Louis Cardinals when his average in 120 games was .304.

Five-foot, four Miller won his place in the Hall as a manager. In 12 seasons with the Yankees beginning in 1918, Huggins won 6 pennants and twice brought his team in second.

Huggins was working with a set of the most wildly individualistic stars ever put on one team. But he won their respect, and eventually their deep affection. He insisted on a strictly business attitude during the game and would not tolerate horseplay while a game was in progress.

Huggins was the manager who first had to discipline the mighty Babe Ruth, and Ruth expressed scorn and disdain for the little fellow at first. But long before Huggins died, Ruth had become devoted to him and he was the only ballplayer to attend him on his deathbed.

Huggins began his professional career with the Cincinnati Reds in 1904, joined the St. Louis Cardinals in 1910 and stayed in baseball until his death at the age of 50 in 1929. As playing manager of the Cards in 1914, Huggins brought them in third, their highest finish since the league was founded in 1876.

Huggins won six pennants for the N. Y. Yankees.

Walter Johnson had fastest pitch ever seen.

WALTER PERRY JOHNSON

WALTER PERRY JOHNSON many baseball men will insist, threw a baseball faster than any other pitcher who ever made the major leagues. There was no machine to measure a pitcher's speed in his day; but Johnson left records that are still unmatched. He pitched more American League games than anyone else, 802, and won more, 416. He set a record by pitching 3 successive complete games (September 4, 5, and 7, 1908) and winning them all by shutout. He also set the record for total shutouts: 113; and for consecutive shutout innings: 56. In his 21-year career with Washington, however, he pitched but 1 no-hit game (an error kept it from being perfect).

Johnson's speed used to make batters and umpires blink in amazement. As a kid in the semi-pro ranks he had trouble finding a catcher to hold him. When he got his full growth (6 feet 1 and 200 pounds) he fired the ball past the batter so fast that many a player would pray he would not have to stand up to him again. He had a terror of injuring a man with his speed and would never deliberately throw at a batter.

One reason Johnson lasted in the big leagues so long (he won 23 games for Washington in his 18th year in the big leagues and 20 games the following year, when he was going on 37 years old) was that he paced himself carefully. With 2 strikes and no balls on a batter he liked to experiment with his curve, which hardly curved at all. And when he had a comfortable lead, he did not fret over men getting on base. Usually, when he really had to, he could bear down hard, and he often struck out the side. He had excellent control and an easy, half-sidearm motion. In his best season (1913) he pitched 51 games, won 36 of them and lost only 7, leading the league. He had 12 seasons in which he won 20 or more games, and 2 in which he won more than 30.

A gentle, high-minded, abstemious and friendly man, Johnson had a thousand friends in baseball. He had two nicknames — Big Train, from the whistling speed of his fast ball, and Barney, because he was supposed to drive his car like Barney Oldfield, the racing driver. But in letters to his friends he always signed himself "Walter."

NAPOLEON LAJOIE nicknamed Larry, does not own

the records that some other hitters do, although he three times led the American League in batting. But his right-handed swing was so smooth and so accurate that many pitchers felt he had no batting weakness at all. He could hit to any field, hit for distance, or bunt to get on base, and in one game, when a pitcher was trying to walk him, he three times reached out one-handed and hit doubles to right field.

As a fielder, Lajoie was one of the finest—on a par with Honus Wagner. His record of 988 fielding chances accepted in a season is the high mark for second basemen in the American League. In 1899, while with the Philadelphia Nationals, he set a mark of 11 putouts in 1 game. In everything he did Larry was noted for his grace. 6 feet 1, weighing almost 200 pounds, Larry, in the infield, was lithe as a cat. At the plate, he was confident, smooth, always the picture hitter. On the basepaths, he stretched many a hit into a double, and long held the record for two-base hits in the American League.

Lajoie had 21 active seasons in the major leagues and left a lifetime batting mark of .339. He finished his baseball career in the minor leagues—with Toronto (where, as manager, he won the only pennant of his career), then with Indianapolis. When he could no longer swing his bat successfully in organized ball he turned to golf, and became a top performer.

THEODORE AMAR LYONS like Walter Johnson

and Mel Ott, spent his entire big-league career with one club and never played in the minors. Ted's club was the Chicago White Sox, whom he joined when he was 22 and where he became manager at the age of 45. In between he did a lot of pitching. For 11 successive seasons he never appeared in fewer than 40 games and in 3 seasons he worked in 50 or more.

In the beginning, Ted was a fast-ball pitcher who could overpower the strong batters. In his first 8 seasons with the White Sox, Ted had 3 seasons in which he won over 20 games, despite the fact that his team dwelt almost permanently in the second division. In the spring of 1931, his ninth season with Chicago, Ted injured his arm so severely that he was never able to attain again the speed he had known as a youth. That year, although he appeared in 42 games, he won but 4 while losing 6, and he never again achieved the 20-victory mark. Yet he continued to pitch for 12 more seasons—and undoubtedly could have made it 15 if he had not taken 3 seasons out with the Marines in World War II.

The secret of Ted's lasting power was his determined acquisition of a knuckle ball, which he practiced sedulously until he could control it. His ability to keep batters off balance with this tantalizing slow pitch, or with a medium change of pace, enabled him to work without undue strain on his injured muscles.

Napoleon Lajoie hit to any field.
Ted Lyons (right), lasted 21 seasons.
Walter Johnson won 416 games.

HENRY EMMETT (HEINIE) MANUSH, born in Tuscumbia, Alabama, was the seventh baseball player born into his family, and the best of them all.

A big left-hander, Heinie was a member of the most murderous outfield ever put together—the Detroit outfield of Cobb, Heilmann, Manush and Fothergill, the back-up man. In 136 games for Detroit in 1926, Heinie's average was .378. Two years later with the St. Louis Browns, Heinie posted the same figure. His lifetime average is .330. His .378 average in 1926 won the league batting crown and he stayed among the batting leaders for 8 years more. In 1928 he and Lou Gehrig led the league in doubles with 47 apiece.

After leaving Detroit, Heinie played with St. Louis and then with Washington, where he stayed 5 seasons. At the age of 35, when his average had fallen off to .273, Heinie was traded to the Red Sox, who kept him one season and then swapped him off to Brooklyn, in the other league. Heinie promptly celebrated his arrival in the curve-ball league by hitting .333 in 132 games. He ended his active career with Pittsburgh in 1939.

Starting with a mining-company team in Utah at the age of 17 and progressing through the minor-league club in Edmonton, Alberta, Heinie spent 22 years as an active ballplayer, then put in a long spell as minor-league manager and big-league scout and coach.

Manush ended his playing days with a lifetime average of .330.

Shortstop of 1914 Miracle Braves was Rabbit Maranville.

WALTER JAMES VINCENT MARANVILLE

called Rabbit, was one of the smallest men ever to play in the big leagues (5 feet 5, and 155 pounds). He was also one of the best liked and one of the funniest. Even his favorite trick of catching a ball with both hands held high against his body—his vest-pocket catch, he called it—seemed like a comedy stunt, for Rab was always doing something to make people laugh. (Once he waded into a hotel pool, caught a goldfish, and took a bite out of it.) But the catch was an important part of his repertoire. He had small hands and wanted to be sure he held on to the ball.

Rabbit was a lion-hearted young man, fast, sure-footed, and aggressive. Before he joined the minor-league team in New Bedford in 1911, young Maranville had played school and sandlot ball as a catcher in Springfield, Massachusetts. He entered organized ball when he was 19 years old and kept on playing until he was 43. Some people say that if he had not broken his leg while sliding home in a spring exhibition game in 1934, he'd be playing yet.

The fans in New Bedford named Maranville Rabbit because of the way he hopped about the infield to collar ground balls. No great man at the plate, he was a fearless and timely hitter who often came through in the clutch. When he moved up to Boston, he joined the team that was to become the Miracle Team in 1914, when Manager George Stallings (with lots of help from Maranville and Johnny Evers) moved them from last place to first place and cleaned up the World Series in 4 straight games.

Maranville starred because he, like Evers, was a team player. He was not out to make records but to win. He had enjoyed the company of ballplayers all his life and he wanted to stay in baseball forever.

Maranville played his final baseball games in 1939, when he was 47, for Albany in the Eastern League, which he managed for a season, and although he had slowed down on the field he was just as aggressive and just as full of fun as when he once crawled between Umpire Hank O'Day's legs at Braves Field to get to the plate.

Eppa Rixey (above),
won 266 games
in twenty years.

Plank (right), had
20 wins or more in eight
seasons out of 17.

Ray Schalk (below),
was thought too small
to be a catcher.

EDWARD STEWART PLANK the great left-hander for Connie Mack's Philadelphia Athletics who won 20 or more games for 8 seasons, never pitched in a minor league. He was a grown man before he went to college and it was while he was at Gettysburg College that he discovered he was a pitcher. (As a boy, the story has it, he amused himself by knocking birds off fences by throwing stones and thus developed the strength and control he needed.) When he joined Connie Mack, he was going on 26 years old. But he stayed with Connie for 14 years, then put in a season with St. Louis in the Federal League and 2 seasons with the St. Louis American League entry.

A solemn man who was accused by sports writers of having no sense of humor, Eddie Plank was the slowest-working pitcher of his day. He would spend so much time between pitches, adjusting his cap, hitching his belt, kicking pebbles out of his way, and then going into a rocker motion that might last a half a minute before he let the ball go toward the plate, that many a batter simply could not keep staring at the mound so long. Then, by the time the ball came down, he failed to focus on it.

Eddie's best season with the Athletics was his twelfth, when he was 37 years old. That year, 1912, he won 26 games and lost but 6. He had 5 shutouts. He had won 26 games in 1904 but lost 17 that year. Eddie was a hard-luck pitcher in many ways, for he lost an unusually large number of close games.

EPPA (JEPTHA) RIXEY was playing for the Culpepper (Virginia) Hurricanes at the age of 7; everyone called him "Eppa" or "Junior." He never heard the name "Jeptha" until he was a grown man pitching in the major leagues, and a newspaperman presented him with it. Eppa liked it so well he adopted it for a middle name.

Eppa, who grew into an enormous young man (6 feet 5 and over 200 pounds), stepped right from the University of Virginia to the roster of the Philadelphia Phillies in 1912. A National League umpire, Charles Rigler, was impressed by the young left-hander's speed and made the deal that brought him into the majors. (It also brought an end to any scouting by umpires, as the other clubs protested.)

Eppa had some trouble at the start, although he won 10 games his first year. In 1913, he won 9 games while losing 5, but the next year he won only 2 while losing 11. In 1915 a new manager, catcher Pat Moran, took over the Phillies, approved of his strong-armed left hander, and helped get him on the track. In 1915, while the Phillies were winning the pennant, Eppa contributed 11 victories. In 1916 he won 22 and lost 10. He was 16 and 21, in a losing cause, in 1917. He entered the army then and served overseas. On his return, he picked up his work-horse chores. But Pat Moran, to whom he gave credit for his development, moved on to Cincinnati and Eppa began to slip. In 1919 he won but 6 games. Next year he won 11 but lost twice as many (he appeared in 43 games). Then he went to Cincinnati and celebrated his reunion with Pat Moran by winning steadily season after season: 19 in 1921; 25 in 1922; 20 in 1923. Indeed, big Eppa did not post a losing season in Cincinnati until 1929, when he was 38 years old. That year, appearing in 35 games, he won 10 and lost 13. He pitched less and less after that—and complained that he was not getting enough work. After a 5 and 5 season in 1932, he finally managed another winning season with a record of 6 won and 3 lost. Then Eppa called it a career and went to selling insurance, a business in which he prospered. His record of 266 victories stood as the best ever attained by a major league left-hander, until Warren Spahn broke it in 1959.

Eppa's fame never matched his skill, perhaps because he never became a World Series hero. In his only World Series game in 1915 he lost to the Boston Red Sox by 1 run, after Harry Hopper, who had hit only 2 home runs all year, bounced 2 lucky homers into the temporary stands in Philadelphia. But Eppa never felt that he was mistreated or ignored by baseball writers or the record keepers. When he was told of his election to the Hall of Fame, he chuckled: "They're really scraping the bottom of the barrel, aren't they?"

Tris Speaker was keystone
in Red Sox dream outfield of
1910-1915. He might
have played for
Pittsburgh if he hadn't
smoked cigarettes.

In 1916 Speaker was
sold to Cleveland and became
manager in 1919.

RAYMOND WILLIAM SCHALK who played for the Chicago White Sox for 17 seasons, never batted over .286 for them except in his final year as a player, when he went to bat twice and got 2 hits, for an average of 1.000. But he was an iron-man catcher and the ablest fielder of his time in the behind-the-bat position. No other American League catcher ever earned a better fielding percentage. Ray caught in 100 games or more for 12 seasons, 11 of them in a row.

Schalk was a little fellow — 5 feet 7, weighing 155 pounds — but he could move around in his position as no one else has before or since. He shares with Bill Dickey the catcher's league record of 3 assists in an inning — and he has one mark that is strictly his own: he made a putout at one time or other at every base — first, second, third, and home. That is because he was always in on every play and ready to move to any part of the field to stay with the ball.

When Schalk joined the White Sox in 1912, after a season with Taylorville and part of one with Milwaukee, Big Ed Walsh, the Chicago spitballer, refused to believe that tiny Schalk could hold his pitches. But Schalk suggested they warm up together and from that time forth, Big Ed wanted no other catcher. "Too small" to block the plate against the husky runners of his day, Schalk developed a method of sending them spinning off his shinguards that was just as effective.

Ray started to play ball when he was invited to catch for the town team in Litchfield, Illinois. He started to play professionally when he was 18 and joined the White Sox when he was 19. He stayed with them until he was 36, serving as manager in his last 2 seasons. He then played a few games for New York, stacking up a record lifetime total (up to his day) of 1721 games as a catcher, and another 30 or so in which he appeared as pinch-hitter.

TRISTRAM E. SPEAKER although hitting was his specialty, was also one of the greatest glove men ever to play center field for a major league team. With the aid of his teammate, Old Cy Young, the Boston pitcher, Speaker practiced hour after hour in the outfield until he learned to tell, by the sound of the bat meeting the ball, and by the timing of Cy Young's swing, just about where the ball was going to fall. With this skill added to his lightning speed, he became a magician in the outfield. He played sometimes almost behind second base and no one has ever matched him in ability to turn his back to the plate and take a fly ball over his shoulder, going away. More than once he robbed hitters of what seemed like certain home runs, once leaping right into the crowd with his back to the diamond and plucking the ball out of the air before he fell into the stands. He tied the American League record for outfield assists (35) in 1909 and tied it again in 1912. There was no such thing as a Texas League single when a big Texan named Speaker was roaming the shallow outfield. He made 2 unassisted double plays in 1918, tying the record.

As a hitter, Spoke led the American League only once, in 1916, after he had been sold to Cleveland because he refused to take a salary cut. That year he batted .386. Most of the time he ran close behind a man named Ty Cobb, who became his close friend and eventually his teammate. Spoke made 11 hits in a row on July 8, 9, and 10 in 1920. And when he completed his career he had set a new mark for two-base hits in the major leagues: 793.

Tris Speaker became manager of the Cleveland Indians in 1919 and held the job until 1926, when he resigned to go first to Washington, then to Philadelphia, and finally to Newark in the International League, where he managed for a season and a half. He led his Cleveland team to only 1 pennant, in 1920, and he took the World Series too, making 8 hits in that Series himself.

JOHN PETER WAGNER is still placed near the top
of the list of all-time All-Stars. In his day, a baseball fan could always start an argument on the subject of whether Ty Cobb or Honus Wagner was the greatest ballplayer alive. Nowadays nearly everyone will name Cobb but in the early 1900's the competition was close. Honus was certainly the greatest shortstop of his era. He could range the whole distance from the deep hole near third to right behind second base to dig ground balls out of the gravel and hurl them (often with a handful of

Honus Wagner
was best
shortstop of
his day.

dirt flying along) hard and fast to first base. Very few men in baseball ever owned a stronger arm than Wagner did and in this department at least he was far ahead of Cobb.

Wagner had an extraordinary pair of hands, with fingers as long as the whole hand of a small man, dangling, some people said, like a bunch of bananas. When he gripped a baseball, the ball looked like a button. Bowlegged as he was, he could fly on the basepaths and on defense he could stand up to the toughest of them. Even the hard-boiled Orioles learned to give the big Dutchman room when he came cannonading down the basepaths. And Ty Cobb once told ruefully of a day when he warned big Honus, "I'm coming down on the next pitch!" This warning, which usually unnerved lesser men, just made Wagner more determined and when Cobb slid in, spikes high, there was Honus to lay the hard side of the ball on his face. "He split my lip for me," said Cobb admiringly.

This was during the only Series when the two great stars played against each other—the World Series of 1909. In that Series Wagner (and Pittsburgh) ran off with the victory. While Cobb stole only 1 base and batted .231, Wagner stole 6 bases and batted .333. (In his first World Series, against Boston, in 1903, Wagner too had been a disappointment, with an average of only .214.)

Wagner started in organized baseball comparatively late in life. He was 21 years old when he broke in with Steubenville, Ohio. His older brother was already a professional ballplayer but Honus had played only as a semi-pro, making his living meanwhile at the coal mines near his home in Carnegie, Pennsylvania. He started out in baseball as a pitcher but gave the job up quickly. "I used to strike out half the side," he would explain (with forgivable exaggeration), "and walk the other half." He played the outfield and infield with equal skill, and played them both in 1895, when he worked with 3 different minor league teams, besides Steubenville: Mansfield, in the Ohio State League; Adrian, in the Michigan State League; and Warren, in the Iron-Oil League.

Ed Barrow bought Wagner from Steubenville in 1896 and took him to play for Paterson, New Jersey, in the Atlantic League. In mid-season, 1897, Wagner was sold to Louisville

Chicago's Big Ed Walsh was greatest of the spitballers.

Big hands on Wagner (left), could hide a baseball.

Zack Wheat hit .375 two seasons in a row, 1923-24.

131

and was transferred, with the best of that team, to Pittsburgh when Louisville dropped out of the National League in 1900. In all his time in the minors, and for his first 17 years in the majors Wagner never owned a batting average of less than .300. Nor did he ever, in the minors or in the majors, until he was 42 years old, play less than 100 games a year. He led the National League in batting eight times—four times in a row (1906-9). He set the National League lifetime mark of games played (2785) and is one of the small group of men who gathered over 3000 hits. As a base stealer, he ranks fourth behind Cobb, Eddie Collins, and Max Carey, in modern lifetime totals.

After he began to slow down a little (he was troubled by rheumatic pains even in his best years), Wagner became manager of Pittsburgh but he resigned after three days. That year, 1917, was his 21st year in the majors and his last as an active player, although he did play some semi-pro ball in Pittsburgh for years afterward. He came back to the Pirates as a coach in 1933 and remained there until his death.

EDWARD AUGUSTIN WALSH was a spitballer,

and probably the best of them all. A big strong right-hander who never seemed to tire, big Ed was willing to pitch every game if he was asked. In 1908, with the Chicago White Sox, he worked in 66 games and won 40 of them. That year he led all the pitchers in the league, pitched the most shutouts, and scored the most strikeouts. He also set the all-time record for innings pitched in one season: 464. And he pitched 3 successive complete games on the schedule, 2 of them on 1 day. He won that double-header, then pitched the next game on the schedule and lost it, although he struck out 15 batters, walked one, and allowed but 4 hits. The very next day, Ed came in as relief pitcher, struck out Lajoie with the bases full, and saved the game.

Ed had won another double-header in 1905 and pitched a no-hit game against Boston in 1911. In his only World Series (the all-Chicago series of 1906) Ed pitched 2 games and won them both, fanning 12 batters in 1 game, and yielding a 2-game total of 8 hits.

Born in Pennsylvania, Ed first played organized ball with Wilkes-Barre in the Pennsylvania State League. He did not realize his full potential as a pitcher until he began to use the spitball, in 1906. The next year he won 24 games for Chicago and, after his 40-victory year in 1908, hit a high mark again with 27 wins in 1911. In 1914, his mighty arm gave out.

ZACHARY DAVIS WHEAT the best outfielder

the Brooklyn Dodgers ever owned, was a fleet-footed and sure-handed young man, raised on a farm in Texas and built rangy and strong as a horse. He was a solid hitter who accomplished more with his bat than any other man who ever graced the Brooklyn roster. He leads all Brooklynites in games played, in times at bat, in total hits, in singles, in doubles, in triples, and in total bases. In 1918, he led the National League in batting with an average of .335. (His top mark was .375, achieved in successive years, 1923 and 1924.) In 1916 he hit safely in 29 consecutive games.

But Zach, also called Buck, was at his best in the outfield. Speeding all over left field on his tiny feet (he wore a size 6 shoe), he specialized in snaring line drives by reaching across his body and taking them backhanded.

Zach started as a professional with Fort Worth in the Texas League when he was almost 19. He played with Shreveport in the Texas League, and with Mobile in the Southern League before he finally came up to Brooklyn in 1909. He did not hit .300 in the minors but as soon as he got to Brooklyn he started to and in the 18 seasons he played there, he hit .300 or better 13 times. He was a left-handed batter, not especially adept at getting down to first at top speed. But once past first he could fly, and he more often than not was able to grab that extra base.

Zack Wheat was Brooklyn's favorite outfielder for 18 seasons: 1909-26.

133

THE GOLDEN AGE

Babe Ruth called his shot in World Series with Cubs, 1932. Here he crosses plate after hitting home run right where he said he would. Lou Gehrig, next at bat, offers Babe congratulations.

BASEBALL HAD ITS GOLDEN AGE BETWEEN THE WORLD WARS. THE ERA OF THE MILLION-DOLLAR OPERATION WAS DOMINATED BY BABE RUTH. NEW LINE-UPS OF HIGHLY-PAID PLAYERS AND MODERN STADIUMS FILLED WITH CAPACITY CROWDS. UNDER THE CONTROL OF A NATIONAL COMMISSIONER, BASEBALL OUTGREW THE LAST VESTIGES OF ITS ROWDY PAST.

GROVER CLEVELAND ALEXANDER known

throughout baseball as Old Pete, tied Christy Mathewson in winning more games than any other National League pitcher who ever lived: 373. In three seasons (1915-17), Old Pete won 31, 33, and 30 games for the Philadelphia Nationals. Then he was traded to the Chicago Cubs and he never had a losing season there. In 1920, his tenth season in the major leagues, he appeared in 46 games for Chicago and won 27.

Although Old Pete spent 20 seasons in the majors with Philadelphia, Chicago, St. Louis, and back in Philadelphia again, and won more than 20 games in 9 of those seasons, he is still remembered best for his relief pitching for the St. Louis Cardinals in the seventh game of the 1926 World Series against the Yankees. Alexander had won the sixth game and, at the age of 39, seemed to have completed his chores. But Manager Hornsby called him in to relieve Jess Haines, who had a blister on his finger, in the seventh inning of the seventh game, with the bases full and Tony Lazzeri at bat. Lazzeri got one blazing foul off Alexander that landed in the left-field stands, just a few feet out of home-run territory. Then Alexander fanned him and went on to save the game and the series. Alexander struck out 2199 men in his major league career, yet this is the one strikeout that is remembered.

No pitcher has ever matched Old Pete's record of 28 victories in his first major league season. Nor has anyone exceeded his record of 16 shutouts in a season. He twice won both ends of double-headers and he posted 21 victories for St. Louis in 1927, the year he turned 40. A master of control and an efficient workman on the mound, Old Pete once completed a major league game in 2 minutes under an hour.

LUCIUS BENJAMIN (LUKE) APPLING is the

only shortstop who ever led the American League in batting. And he did it twice—in 1936 with an average of .388 and in 1943 with an average of .328. Luke also played more games at shortstop than any other player in the history of the major leagues. During the 20 years he played with the White Sox, he played shortstop in 2,218 games, made 2,749 hits and appeared as third baseman or pinch hitter in 204 more. But he is remembered today for frequent injuries to himself and for his ability to foul-off pitches by the dozen.

Luke's penchant for fouling-off pitches derived from his habit of punching most of his hits to the opposite field. He tired out many a pitcher that way.

Born in High Point, North Carolina, Luke became a football and baseball star at Oglethorpe University in Atlanta, Ga. He signed with the Atlanta club of the Southern Association and was soon sought after by major-league clubs. At first fans booed him because he booted so many ground balls. But he later showed the fans the best fielding they had ever seen at his position.

Grover Cleveland Alexander won 30 games 3 years in a row.

Appling played more games at short than any player in history.

GORDON STANLEY COCHRANE a solidly built

young man of medium height, was one of the fastest men ever to crouch behind the bat. He was aggressive, smart, and fiery—a natural leader and a never-say-die competitor. He led the American League six times in total putouts for a catcher; and he hit the ball solidly and often. In 1932, with Philadelphia, he hit 23 home runs. His lifetime batting average was

Frankie Frisch, a tough customer, at 1934 World Series.

Grover Cleveland Alexander, age 40, won 21 games in 1927.

In World War II Cochrane led U. S. Navy team at Great Lakes Station.

.320 and his top mark was .357, attained in 1929. He caught 100 or more games in 11 successive seasons.

Sold to the Detroit Tigers in 1933 for a price in excess of $100,000, Mickey became manager there and led the club to its first pennant in 25 years in 1934. He won another pennant, plus the World Championship, in 1935. His playing career came to an untimely end when he suffered a fractured skull when hit by a pitched ball on May 25, 1937. The previous season, he had spent many weeks on the sidelines, suffering from a succession of injuries and ailments, including trouble with his eyes and stomach. This accident put him off the diamond for good. The following year, when a new owner took over the Tigers, Cochrane was dropped as manager; but he came back in later years to join the Philadelphia Athletics as coach and then to become general manager. In the meantime he served in the Navy during the war and coached a first-rank baseball team for the Great Lakes Naval Training Station.

JOSEPH EDWARD CRONIN could play almost any baseball position. During his 20 active seasons in the major leagues, this solid, lantern-jawed Irishman played shortstop, all three bases, and the outfield. Then, to prove that his baseball was not all in his muscles, he served as player-manager, nonplaying manager, general manager, and finally as American League president.

The Washington Senators bought Cronin halfway through the 1928 season. Joe made good, after half a dozen false starts.

In his first full year with Washington, Joe hit .282. That was the lowest mark he made for a complete year in his entire stay with Washington. In 1930, Joe hit .346, the high mark of his career. As a fielder he led all American League shortstops in 1932 and 1933.

Joe, an aggressive yet good-natured man, was a natural field boss, always alert to the play that was in the making, respected by his mates, and an instinctive strategist. After 2 seasons as manager (he won 1 pennant) he was sold (for a quarter million dollars, it was said) to the Boston Red Sox. He managed Boston for 13 seasons.

Joe won only 1 pennant with the Red Sox, in 1946, but he had his team in contention most of the time. Next to the 1946 pennant, Joe is proudest of the time in 1939 when the Red Sox—always the Yankees' bitterest foes, since the Yanks "stole" the entire Red Sox line-up, beginning with Babe Ruth, in the 1920's—took 5 straight from New York.

JAY HANNA DEAN called Dizzy, was the son of an itinerant cotton picker. He was a strong right-hander with a fine three-quarter overhand motion. His fast ball smoked and his curve ball (or "crooky" as he called it) seemed to snap its tail in the batter's face. He started playing formalized baseball in the army at Fort Sam Houston, Texas. A train conductor wrote to Branch Rickey of the St. Louis Cardinals about him and Rickey sent a scout to look the boy over. On the basis of the scout's report Rickey invited Dean to a tryout camp, took one look at the 6-feet-3 youngster with the devil-may-care attitude, and signed him to play for St. Joseph. Success came to Dean at once, and almost immediately earned him his nickname, for his behavior in St. Joseph was eccentric enough to delight even the most jaded sports writer. But Dean was no eccentric on the mound. In his first season in organized ball he won 17 games and struck out 134 batters for St. Joseph. He won 30 games for the St. Louis Cardinals in 1934 and 28 in 1935. He set a National League strikeout record for his day of 17 in a game and he led the league in strikeouts 4 seasons in a row. He also shared a minor league hitting record, along with 7 other players: He got 2 base hits in a single inning one day.

An injury shortened Dizzy's career, when he had to change his pitching motion to favor a sore toe hit by a line drive in the 1937 All-Star Game. His arm went lame on him then and he never regained his speed. His cunning kept him in the big leagues, however, for another 3 years. He closed out his career with a flash of glory when in 1947, with the St. Louis American League team, after he had become a highly popular baseball broadcaster, he pitched 4 innings in the final game, allowed no runs and got a hit in his only time at bat.

Joe Cronin (left), was a
topnotch tennis player before
he joined the Pittsburgh
Pirates. They sold him
to Washington, where he
became a great shortstop
and manager.

Left to right are
President Roosevelt,
Clark Griffith, Washington
owner; Joe Cronin, and
Giants' Bill Terry.

Dizzy Dean had
seen his best days
when he joined
the Chicago Cubs
in 1938.

But Dean could still fog
the fast one through
often enough to win a few
games for the Cubs.

At right, Dizzy Dean
at the height of his fame:
30-game winner
for St. Louis, 1934.

WILLIAM MALCOLM DICKEY never played for any major league club except the New York Yankees, but he did a great deal of catching for them. A long-legged, long-armed, broad-shouldered lad from Arkansas, Dickey was unusually tall for a catcher and had to squat a long way to get down behind the bat.

When Bill joined the Yankees at the age of 20, he had already done a lot of catching in the minors. In 1939, with the Yankees, he caught 140 games, and he holds the record of 13 seasons in which he caught 100 games or more. Bill could hit big-league pitching too. In his first full year with the Yankees, he hit .324. In 16 seasons (with time out for war service) Bill fell below .300 in batting only five times.

Although Bill was not fast on his feet, he was fast-thinking and he was quick to diagnose plays. He pounced on bunts like a cat and blocked the plate without fear. He caught 125 games without a passed ball in 1931 and he shares the major league record for catchers of 3 assists in 1 inning. Six times he led all catchers in putouts and three times in assists. In 1941, he made an unassisted double play.

It was his big bat rather than his steadiness behind the plate that kept Bill in the line-up so often. In 2 consecutive games in 1937 he hit home runs with the bases full. He hit a total of 29 that year. He also set a record (since tied) by making 4 hits in 1 World's Series game (October 5, 1938), and another record by batting in 5 runs in 1 World's Series game (October 2, 1936).

JOSEPH PAUL DIMAGGIO the pride of the New York Yankees, might have become the pride of Boston, or some other city, had there been any baseball executive besides George Weiss willing to take a chance on Joe's "bad" knee. But other clubs shied away from Joe after his left knee snapped out of joint one day and forced him to spend 6 weeks on crutches. The Yankee management, however, who had been impressed as everyone else had been by Joe's great play for the San Francisco Seals in the Pacific Coast League, sent Joe to a doctor and received assurance that the injury was not permanent. So Joe became a Yankee and never played for any other major league club.

Starting with the New York Yankees in 1936, after 3 full seasons (and the tail end of another) with the Seals, Joe played 10 full seasons with the Yankees, spent three years in military service and in 1949 played about half the regularly scheduled games. In this year, he was suffering from a recurrence of a bone spur on his heel that had threatened to end his career a year earlier. He was no longer "pulling" the ball in the manner he had made famous. Every time he ran, pain knifed through his foot. Yet he hit .346 that season, collected 14 home runs, and played in all 5 World Series games.

Joe was essentially a long-ball hitter. He had about the widest stance of anyone in the big leagues in his day and strode forward just a few inches when he swung at the pitch. Like most of the great modern sluggers, Joe was a wrist hitter and could wait until the last second before snapping his bat around to drive the ball to deep left. His fielding was a delight to watch, for he covered ground with a smooth loping stride and seemed able to encompass the whole outfield if need be. He had a strong arm, until age and injury weakened it somewhat, and threw many a runner out at the plate from deep center field. The admiration of nearly all his contemporaries, Joe set a style for Yankee outfielders and for Yankee hitters — to perform the job in workmanlike, aggressive, and consistent manner, without flamboyance and without letup, and to play to win.

Joe had a lifetime batting average of .325 and twice led the league in batting averages of .381 (1939) and .352 (1940). His high mark in the minors was .398.

Joe's most famous batting record was his hitting safely in 56 consecutive games, a mark he made in 1941. But in the Pacific Coast League 8 years earlier he had hit safely in 61 consecutive games.

ROBERT WILLIAM ANDREW FELLER

Cleveland's fireball pitcher, came into the big leagues straight from school, when he was not yet eighteen years old. (The

Bill Dickey of the
Yankees caught over 100
games 13 years in a
row. Note here how fingers
of his "meat" hand are
closed, but relaxed,
to avoid fracture.

New York Murderers' Row,
1936: Dickey, .362;
Gehrig, .354; DiMaggio, .323;
Lazzeri, .287. This was
DiMaggio's first
season; Gehrig's 14th.

Joe DiMaggio
was a pull hitter
with a wide stance and
short stride.

Joe DiMaggio's single scored three runs this time, thanks to Joe's miraculous slide, plus two errors.

Not even DiMaggio
could get a hit off Feller
this day. Bobby is
throwing a no-hitter.

DiMaggio crosses
plate (above) in 45th
game of 1941
hitting streak.

Cleveland team gave him a job in the concession department to keep him handy before he was ready to put a uniform on.) Ballplayers who faced him then said he was the fastest man since Johnson and there are even a few who think he might have been a mite faster. Johnson, although a modest man, could not agree that young Bob threw faster than he had thrown; but nearly everyone agreed that Bob was surely next best.

Feller's fast ball, like Johnson's, came down so fast that many a batter lost sight of it and on that account the hitters, during Feller's best years, stood "on top of their spikes" in the batter's box, ready to get out of the way in a hurry. Feller's trick of looking everywhere but at the plate when he was preparing to deliver the ball increased the batters' uneasiness.

Had Feller not lost three full seasons because of his war service, his records might have topped them all, for he was at his best when he joined the Navy, having completed consecutive seasons when he won 24, 27, and 25 games. After the war, in 1946 and 1947, he won 26 and 20 games respectively and in 1948 he helped the Indians win their first pennant in many years by posting 19 victories. Unlike Johnson, Bob Feller had a magnificent curve ball that came down nearly as fast as his hard one. His motion was "big" and loose and overpowering, with a deep pump and a mighty stride that in itself was almost enough to make a hitter quail. On April 16, 1940, Feller opened the season with a no hit 1-0 victory over Chicago, the first no-hit opening day game in the American League since 1900. Six years later, on another cool April day, when he was "not feeling right" he pitched another no-hitter against New York in the Yankee stadium. On October 2, 1938, he broke Rube Waddell's strikeout record by fanning 18 Detroit Tigers in the first game of a double-header. In this game he fanned six batters in a row, to tie the league record. In his first season in organized baseball, he had fanned 16 Red Sox batters during the first game of an August double-header.

In 1946 Feller established the modern season record of 348 strikeouts and for seven seasons he struck out more

Even oldtimers agreed that Bob Feller
was nearly as fast as Walter Johnson.

batters than any other pitcher in the league. Three times (1941-46-47) he led the league in shutouts, twice tied for the lead (1939 and 1940), and in 1940 he topped the league in earned-run average (2.62).

Feller pitched in but one World Series (against Boston in 1948) and could not win a game. In All-Star competition, however, he was nearly invincible. Between 1939 and 1946 he pitched in four All-Star games, a total of 11 innings, and allowed but one earned run.

JAMES EMORY FOXX despite a friendly, outgoing
nature, was known as "the Beast" in organized baseball, simply because he seemed something more than human at the plate. Not quite 6 feet tall, he had a chest and a pair of arms that would have looked normal on a giant; and he could use the muscles hidden there to rocket a batted ball as far as any human being has ever done before or since.

Jimmy was one of the Philadelphia Athletics' most famous graduates and he was discovered by an older graduate of the same club: Frank "Home Run" Baker. When Baker first saw Foxx, Jimmy was a catcher with Easton (Maryland) in the Eastern Shore League and he was only 16 years old. At Baker's urging, Connie Mack signed Jimmy when the boy was 17, let him go to bat 9 times (during which Jimmy got 6 hits), then put him in Providence to learn some other position besides catcher. Mack already had a catcher named Cochrane. Jimmy learned to play first base and third base and in 1928, at the age of 20, became one of Connie's regulars. He batted .328 that year and got 13 home runs. Not for 14 years did he hit so few home runs again. In 1932, he led the American League with 58 home runs; in 1933, with 48; in 1935 (tie), with 36; and in 1939, with 35. Only Babe Ruth, in his major league career, hit more home runs than Jimmy did. Foxx collected 534.

Jimmy's drives were not long flies. He hit the ball on the nose and drove it straight and hard. (He actually did, in batting practice, hit a young pitcher on the skull with a drive and send the young man out of the big leagues.)

Jimmy Foxx
with the Red Sox
played first,
third, pitcher,
catcher and
outfield.

In 1929, the three sluggers at right, Foxx, Cochrane, and Simmons, won the championship for Connie Mack's A's.

Jimmy Foxx, above, hit 58 homers in 1932 and 50 in 1938.

Frankie Frisch, shown here as
player and manager, graduated from
John McGraw's tough Giants
to lead the St. Louis Gashouse Gang.

Jimmy got at least 1 home run in every World Series he ever played in: with Philadelphia in 1929 (2 home runs), 1930, and 1931. After he was sold to the Boston Red Sox in 1936, Jimmy hit 41 home runs his first season there and 2 seasons later hit 50. He was the American League batting leader in 1933, with .356. He also led the league in 1938, when he was with Boston, with .349. Before he was through, he had played pitcher as well as catcher and had become an able performer at both first and third base. He still holds the record for the number of consecutive years in which a batter hit 30 or more home runs. Jimmy did it 12 times.

FRANK FRANCIS FRISCH a switch hitter known as

the Fordham Flash, was no college-boy athlete. He was rough-and-ready, aggressive, and tough as they came, cast in the image of John McGraw, a man he greatly admired and the big-league manager he first played for. He was the ideal leader of the team with which he earned his greatest fame—the great St. Louis Gashouse Gang of the 1930's.

While Frankie was with McGraw, he played second base, third base, and shortstop and starred at each position. Eventually he settled to second base, where he was recognized as one of the game's greatest. But right to the end of his active career he was ready to fill in at either of the other spots as well. Frankie was the "holler guy" in the infield—the man who could cajole, encourage, even enrage his teammates to play their best; and he was equally vociferous on the bench, where he took a vocal part in every maneuver on the field.

Although Frankie never led the league in batting, his lifetime major league average is .316 and his high mark was .348, made in 1923, with the Giants, when he led the league in total base hits. In 1924, while with the Giants, he once made 6 hits in 6 consecutive times at bat.

Because Frankie ate and slept baseball, he was born to be a manager. He took charge both on the field and off—and sometimes after he had been banished from the field. (A favorite trick, when he was manager and had been ordered from the field for overenthusiastic protests, was to lie flat on the dugout floor and run the team from there.)

Henry Louis Gehrig,
Yankee Iron Horse,
played in 2,130
consecutive games.

Lou Gehrig here is wearing the uniform of his "Larrupin Lous," barnstorming team that toured with Ruth's "Bustin Babes."

Lou Gehrig wept when
60,000 fans cheered him in his
final appearance, 1939.

Above, Gehrig makes
a putout on Joe Vosmik
in June, 1936.

Frank was a shortstop at Fordham and while he was at college played shortstop for the New York Athletic Club every Sunday. He was signed by McGraw while still in college and never played in the minors. It was McGraw who discovered he could play second and third better than short and it was McGraw who instilled the win-the-game-if-it-kills-you spirit in the youngster.

Frankie three times led the National League in stolen bases. He played in 8 World Series, 4 with New York and 4 with St. Louis. In his 2 All-Star Games, he made 4 hits in 7 times at bat.

HENRY LOUIS GEHRIG played more games in a row (for the New York Yankees) than anyone in major league baseball. Lou, who was given nicknames that never stuck (Larrupin' Lou, Buster) was finally called, in print at least, the Iron Horse, for he seemed indestructible. Despite colds, bruises, pains, aches, and even despite the crippling disease that finally killed him, Lou Gehrig put his uniform on and at least made an appearance in more consecutive games than most people ever see: 2130.

A big, rugged, quiet, and determined man, Lou began to play first base regularly for the New York Yankees on June 1, 1925 and did not leave the starting line-up until May 2, 1939, when he took himself out of the game because he was too ill to play ever again. He died 2 years later. Because he was Babe Ruth's teammate, he seemed always to be coming in second to Ruth and never achieved quite the headlines that Babe did. But his batting feats were nearly as miraculous. Five times he hit more than 40 home runs in a season and twice led the league with 49. He hit 4 home runs in 3 consecutive World Series games against St. Louis in 1928. He set an American League record for most runs batted in (184) in a single season. He hit 4 consecutive home runs in 1 game on June 3, 1932; and he set a major league lifetime record for most home runs with the bases full: 23. He led the American League in batting in 1934 with a mark of .363.

Gehrig signed with New York in 1923 and was farmed to

Hartford for most of the next 2 seasons. Then Lou moved in at first base and hit 20 home runs and batted .295. His average did not fall below .300 again until 1938, when he hit .295 again. In this, his last full season in the game, he hit 29 home runs.

A legend before he left the game, and a full-blown hero afterward, Lou has a street named after him in New York, where he had been a high-school football player as a boy.

CHARLES GEHRINGER who played second base for the Detroit Tigers for 16 full seasons and part of 3 more, became known as "the Mechanical Man" because he always did his work the same way—perfectly. A quiet young man from a farm near Fowlerville, Michigan, Gehringer signed with the Detroit Tigers before he was 21, played a few games for them in 1924 and 1925, performed in 2 minor-league towns and then put in the rest of his career with Detroit.

There was no flamboyance in Gehringer either on or off the field. Even during his active days fans were often surprised to be reminded that he was the best second baseman in the league, for it was Gehringer's habit to stay out of the spotlight and to do nothing to earn himself extra notice in the newspapers.

Gehringer had his first great year at bat in 1934, when the Tigers won their first pennant in 25 years. Charley hit .356 that season. But three seasons later he made it .371 and led the American League. He was named the Most Valuable Player in the league that year. In his 19 seasons with Detroit, he hit for less than .300 only five times (in his first season, 1924, when he played in only 5 games, he batted .545). In 3 successive All-Star Games, he had exactly the same batting average: .667. In the fourth he hit .600.

HENRY BENJAMIN GREENBERG was hitting home runs for Detroit when Babe Ruth was still hitting them for the Yankees and one year big Hank nearly tied Babe's record. He hit 58 homers in 1938.

No right-handed batter ever hit more home runs in a season than Hank Greenberg did. (Jimmy Foxx hit just as many.) With Detroit he hit better than .300 in every full season he

Greenberg, right, receiving
Most Valuable Player
award from Judge Landis, 1936.

Gehringer (scoring) used
to "take" the first pitch, he said,
"so the pitcher could start even."

played, except the last one, 1946, when he hit only .277. (In 1941, when he interrupted his baseball career to enter the service, he played but 19 games.) And in that final full season, despite the falling off of his average, he still contrived to knock 44 fair balls out of the park, leading the league for the fourth time (with one tie).

Hank Greenberg was not the fanciest-fielding of first basemen. In two seasons he led the league in errors. But he also managed to lead the league three times in putouts and twice in assists. He was a quiet, determined, workmanlike player who was always putting out his best for the team. He once played out a ball game with two bones broken in his wrist. He played the outfield toward the end of his career in Detroit but when he was sold to Pittsburgh in 1947 he went back to playing first base—and hit 25 home runs.

When he had become too old to play, Hank moved to the business end of baseball and, teamed with Bill Veeck, had a hand in bringing pennants first to Cleveland and then to Chicago.

ROBERT MOSES GROVE called Lefty, was one of the fastest pitchers who ever lived; when he started playing ball for money, in Midland, Maryland, he played first base, because there was not a catcher in the area who could hold his fiery fast ball. When a boy was found who could hold Grove's pitches, Bob gained fame quickly and graduated from Midland to Martinsburg, West Virginia, and then to the Baltimore Orioles. With the Orioles he became the best pitcher in the International League and he was sold to the Philadelphia Athletics for $100,600. (The extra $600 was added to the check to make the price a record. Babe Ruth had been sold to the Yankees for $100,000.)

It took Lefty Grove 2 seasons to become a successful big-league pitcher, for he was careless at first of his control. But once having won 20 games in 1927 (appearing in 51 games), he went 6 more seasons without winning less than 20. For 3 straight seasons Lefty led the American League in both earned-run average and won-lost percentage. And after he injured his arm and was sold to the Boston Red Sox (for more than that $100,600) he developed a fine curve and "fork-ball" change of pace that gave him 6 more winning and 2 break-even seasons until he had finally attained his goal of 300 victories.

CHARLES LEO HARTNETT was one of the most talkative and most aggressive men who ever played major league baseball—and one of the best liked. He caught on quickly with the Chicago Cubs (after a season in Worcester, in the Eastern League), because the Cub pitching star, Grover Cleveland Alexander, took a liking to him and insisted that he be his catcher. Before long the fans and the players all shared Alexander's preference, for Gabby had a way with him. He would strut to his position like a man about to announce his claim to ownership of the ball park, greet opponents and fans with an all-inclusive wave of his big hand, and then drive his clenched fist into the air to indicate that the battle was on.

Gabby always played with every ounce of his strength. Despite his size (he was one of the heartiest eaters in baseball), he never loafed, never looked for the easy way, never failed to try for that extra advantage.

He was sure-handed, cool, and confidence-inspiring. In all his career with the Cubs he dropped but 3 high fouls behind the plate. He seldom caught fewer than 100 games for the Cubs. But when he had to lay aside his catching gear one year because of a sore arm, he was kept on as a pinch-hitter and drove in 9 runs in 22 times at bat. In 1937, he hit .354 in 110 games, the high mark of his career. In 1930, he hit 37 home runs.

Gabby was appointed to manage the Cubs in 1938, when there were 25 games left to play and the Cubs were 6½ games off the pace. With Gabby in the lead, the Cubs captured 21 victories and took the pennant. Gabby himself won the decisive game by driving out a home run in a game with Pittsburgh, with the score tied, 2 men out, and 2 strikes on him.

ROGERS HORNSBY is generally regarded as the greatest right-handed batter who ever played big-league ball. His unique batting stance—feet together, standing as far back and as far away from the plate as the batter's box would allow—has seldom been imitated with any real success. In the era of the

Lefty Grove, who pitched for both the Red Sox and Athletics, won 300 games in 17 seasons.

With the A's, Lefty was a fireballer. With the Red Sox, he turned "cute" and lasted until he was 41.

Charles Hartnett, Cubs'
catcher, was called "Gabby"
because of his chatter.
He kept fans and teammates
stirred to fever heat.

Gabby managed the Chicago
Cubs for three seasons (1938-40)
and played first base for a
time. In 1937 he batted .354.

Rogers Hornsby, called the
game's greatest right-handed batter,
stood as far from the plate as
the batting box allowed.
He batted .424 in 1924.

Above, Hornsby hits a homer
in a practice game in Los Angeles
after the Cubs bought him from
Boston for $250,000.

lively ball no one ever hit more often than Hornsby did. From 1921 to 1925, he never hit for an average of less than .384 and he three times hit over .400. In 1924, he attained the "modern" batting record of .424.

Hornsby was a great fielder too, with a quick and accurate "double-play" throw, made right across his chest without shifting his feet—the most difficult throw for a second baseman to make. Indeed it was his fielding (when he was a shortstop in Denison, Texas) that first attracted the attention of big-league scouts. When he came up to the St. Louis Cardinals in 1915, he choked his bat and hit from a crouch, bending close to the plate as the ball came in. It was not until he had adopted his far-back, free-swinging style that he began to attain high batting marks. With the Cardinals, he played shortstop, first base, and third base before he even tried out at second, where he was to become the top performer of his day.

In his first full season at St. Louis, after he had learned to change his batting posture, and began to hit to all fields, shifting with the pitch, he made a mark of .313. For his remaining time in the big leagues he had only three seasons under .300 and he had just as many full seasons over .400. He won the National League batting championship six times in a row, and seven times altogether.

CARL OWEN HUBBELL is the only major league player of the post-1900 era to earn the old-fashioned nickname of "King." He also became known to sports writers as the "Meal Ticket" because of his reliability: in his 16 years with the New York Giants, the only major league team he ever pitched for, Hubbell had only 1 losing season. That was in 1940, when he won 11 and lost 12.

Hubbell, a tall, skinny left-hander with beetling eyebrows, was a deliberate worker on the mound. His favorite weapon was his "screwball" pitch—a reverse curve thrown by turning the thumb in rather than out on delivery, so that when thrown by a left-hander the ball breaks in toward a left-handed hitter.

Hubbell pitched a no-hit game against Pittsburgh in 1929 and pitched an 18-inning shutout against St. Louis in 1933 in which he did not issue a base on balls. In 1936, after his arm had gone bad and he had an operation to remedy it, he threw 16 victories in a row, and 8 more to begin the next year. In 1933, he pitched 46⅓ consecutive shutout innings for a National League record. He had 10 shutouts that year.

His best-remembered feat, however, is his striking out the pride of the American League in the 1934 All-Star Game. Babe Ruth, Lou Gehrig, Jimmy Foxx, Al Simmons, and Joe Cronin all went down on strikes before the screwball wizard. It took only 6 screwballs to dispose of Ruth and Gehrig.

KENESAW MOUNTAIN LANDIS is credited with having saved organized baseball from collapse after the Black Sox scandals of 1919. Judge Landis was made First Commissioner of Baseball and set about purging the game of the men who were undertaking to corrupt it. He ruled a number of players out of baseball for life and even disciplined those who played with such men on teams outside his jurisdiction. The result was that, within a year or two, organized baseball's face had been thoroughly scrubbed and the whole tone of the game—both as a business and as a spectacle—was improved.

Judge Landis also made a point of seeing that the spectators received fair treatment. Once he ordered the entire proceeds of a World Series game donated to charity because the fans felt that the game had been called off, when the score was tied, without good reason. He made it his business to investigate the fairness of player contracts and to prevent, when he could, the unfair "hiding" of players in the minor leagues until the parent club was ready for them. By declaring such men free agents, Landis broke up a system that had sometimes resulted in denying a talented player a chance to sell his services for the best price.

Before becoming Commissioner of Baseball, Judge Landis, as a Federal District Judge, had heard the suit brought by the "outlaw" Federal League in 1915 against the National and American Leagues, who, the Federal League charged, were conspiring to limit competition. Landis, in order to see the matter settled peaceably, postponed any decision until the

Giants' Carl Hubbell
on May 4th, 1937 (below),
pitched his 19th win
in a row, over two seasons.

Hubbell's best pitch
was his screwball or reverse
curve, which never came
when the batter expected it.

Kenesaw Mountain Landis,
a small but commanding figure,
liked dramatic poses. He
never wore his hat for pictures.

Landis was death on the
"farm" system, but in spite of him
baseball club owners built
extensive holdings.

The only time Joe McCarthy wore a major-league uniform was when he led Cubs, Yankees, and Red Sox.

McCarthy won one pennant with the Cubs and eight with the New York Yankees.

older leagues had bought out the interests of the Federal League club owners. It was his circumspect handling of this matter that prompted the club owners to turn to him in 1920, when the Black Sox scandal seemed to be destroying public confidence in the game's honesty.

JOSEPH VINCENT McCARTHY until he was made manager of the Chicago National League Club in 1926, had never even set foot inside a big-league dugout. Joe played second base, third base, shortstop, and outfield in the American Association and that was as close as he ever came. He first made his reputation as manager of Louisville, in the American Association, where he won 1 pennant and finished in the first division six times out of seven tries.

Joe became one of the greatest of managers because he knew how to take charge. He did not bully his men, as managers of the old school liked to do, nor was he one of the boys, as a few of his own predecessors had been. He could hold a loose rein on men like Grover Cleveland Alexander or Babe Ruth or Hack Wilson and be tough as a prison guard with some fresh kid who did not feel like trying. He had firm faith in his own judgment of players and let no question of sentiment or public pressure sway him when he thought it was time to let a man go. In Chicago, he turned the Cubs from a second-division team to a pennant winner in 4 seasons. 2 years later he came to New York, and within 2 more years brought his Yankees in first to beat the Cubs out of a World Championship.

With the New York Yankees McCarthy established a team reputation for "class"—which included dignity on the field and off, a minimum of argument with umpires, strict decorum and neat dress in public, and winning baseball at the Yankee Stadium. Under Joe McCarthy, the New York Yankees won 8 pennants and 7 World Championships.

WILLIAM BOYD McKECHNIE a switch-hitting infielder, was called "Deacon" because he looked and acted like one. A soft-spoken, religious man, who avoided strong drink, Bill was still tough-fibered enough to hold a rein on the

Deacon Bill McKechnie won pennants in three major league cities but ended his career as a coach.

most rambunctious player. It was his skill at managing that won him a place in the Hall of Fame, for his actual play was no more than average. He is the only manager who ever won pennants in three different major league cities.

Only once in his life did Bill hit over .300. That was in 1914 when he was playing third base for Indianapolis in the Federal League, where Edd Roush was also playing. He and Roush moved together to Newark, where Bill became manager; and they went to the Giants together and then were traded at the same time to the Reds. By this time most of McKechnie's major league career was behind him. After starting in the Pennsylvania-Ohio-Maryland League, Bill had signed with Pittsburgh in 1907 and played but three games (at third base and second base) before being sent down to Canton of the Ohio-Pennsylvania League. In 1911, he was back with Pittsburgh for two and a half seasons, put in part of two seasons with St. Paul in the American Association, went to the Boston Braves as an outfielder and was quickly waived to the New York Yankees, where manager Frank Chance kept him on despite his feeble work at the bat. "He has brains," Chance explained.

Bill had six more seasons in the majors as a player. In July 1922, he was made manager of the Pirates when the team was in sixth place, finished the season in fourth place and won the pennant three seasons later. In 1927 he joined St. Louis as a coach and in 1928 he was made manager and won the pennant. He was sent to Rochester that same year because he failed to win a single game in the World Series. He had his Rochester team in first place when the Cardinals called him back. The next year he moved to Boston and, after eight lean years with the Boston Braves, he returned to Cincinnati and won two pennants in a row, 1939 and 1940. In 1946, he ended his managerial career and signed as a coach with the Cleveland Indians. He went with Lou Boudreau to Boston, for two seasons, before retiring, at the age of 66, after 48 years in the game.

MELVIN THOMAS OTT never played minor league ball in his life, and spent his playing career with one club.

Mel Ott joined the Giants when he was 17 and spent his whole career with them.

John McGraw of the Giants turned Ott into an outfielder, helped teach him how to run, and let him concentrate on his strong, level batting swing. Ott's peculiar stance at the plate was entirely his own. He stood with feet far apart, and stepped forward only a few inches as he swung. But he made that step by lifting his front foot (the right foot) high in the air and bringing it sharply down just before he met the ball. This motion, he said, gave him extra leverage. It did indeed result in many home runs, for Ott "pulled" every pitch, and the short right-field fence in the Polo Grounds seemed made to order for him.

Ott set National League all-time records in home runs (511), runs scored (1859), and runs batted in (1860). He also set the league mark for bases on balls (1708). In 8 seasons he hit 30 or more home runs and one year (1929) he hit 42. He was a first-rate outfielder too, despite the heavily muscled legs that helped power his bat but kept him from being a speedster in the field. His mighty arm, and his skill at playing caroms off the short Polo Grounds fences, made him into a menace to opposing runners. One year (1935) he led all right fielders in the league in fielding percentage. He was manager of the Giants from 1942 to 1948.

HERBERT JEFFERIS PENNOCK the great left-handed pitcher (and switch batter), is another player who spent all his adult life in organized baseball. He pitched in the American League for 22 seasons, with Philadelphia, Boston, and New York, then became a coach with the Boston Red Sox, then supervisor of their farm system, and finally general manager of the Philadelphia Phillies. In between, he had played in the International League, with Providence for part of 1915 and with Buffalo for part of the following season.

A control pitcher chiefly, who would not throw 10 fast balls in a game, Pennock pitched 7⅓ perfect innings in the World Series of 1923 for the Yankees against the Pittsburgh Pirates and he never lost a World Series game (he won 5). In his 10 World Series appearances, Pennock gave up only 8 walks. He pitched both sidearm and overhand and could make a ball curve both ways. His change of pace was as good as any in the

Herb Pennock won five World Series games and never lost one. He pitched 22 seasons.

league in his day, so his lack of a fast ball did not deter him.

When he was 40 years old, Pennock brought his active career to a close but in that final year (1934) Herb worked in 30 games as relief pitcher for the Red Sox and posted an earned-run average of 3.05.

EDGAR CHARLES (SAM) RICE of the Washington Senators hit 182 singles in 1925, to establish an American League record, and he got a share of another record when he went to bat 600 times or more in 8 seasons. Except for these feats, however, Sam made few appearances in the record books. Yet he hit the ball solidly and consistently for 18 seasons with the Senators, and he was ranked among the game's top outfielders for more than a decade. He was fast, sharp-eyed, deadly on fly balls, and he owned a rifle arm.

Sam started out as a pitcher, like most strong-armed youths. But he could not establish himself on the mound. He had 1 winning season (9—2) with Petersburg in the Virginia League, and 1 losing season (11—12), in which he struck out 153 batters. With Washington he pitched 1 game at the end of his career and won that. When he joined the Senators in July 1915 he found a team that was loaded with pitchers—led by the best of them all, Walter Johnson.

By the middle of the next season Sam (so christened by a sportswriter who couldn't remember his real name) was trying to argue himself into the line-up. Finally Manager Clark Griffith, having already used Walter Johnson as a pinch-hitter and part-time outfielder, let Sam pinch-hit. (In 1915 he had hit 3 home runs in 8 times at bat.) Sam immediately displayed his value at the plate and got himself a full-time job as an outfielder. In his first game as a regular, Rice hit a double, a triple, and a single, fired several balls in on a trolley wire from right field, and covered his area as if he had been raised there. In the final 13 games of the 1916 season, he got 20 hits in 54 times at bat. The next year he displayed a new talent—blazing speed on the basepaths—and before he grew old he had earned the nick-name "Man o' War."

In Sam's 19 full seasons with Washington, his batting average dropped under .300 only 4 times. In 1916 he hit .299; in

Sam Rice
was called Sam
because a writer
forgot his
real name
was Edgar.

Jackie Robinson (left)
batted .342 for the
Dodgers in 1949.

(Above) Jackie Robinson revived
the art of stealing home.

1922 he hit .295; in 1927, .297; in 1933, .294. In 1934 he was sold to the Cleveland Indians and hit .293 in 97 games.

What most people recall about Sam Rice is his tremendous skill in the field. And perhaps the greatest feat of his life—and possibly the greatest play ever made at the Washington ball park—was Sam's leaping catch of a sure home run that big Earl Smith of Pittsburgh popped into the centerfield stands in the 1925 World Series. Sam had been moved to center for this Series, to make room for another slugger. When the Smith blow came his way, he timed it perfectly, leaped high into the air, nailed the ball and sailed right over the low fence into the laps of the bleacher bugs. One of the fans snatched the ball away from Sam, but the umpire ruled it a fair catch and the fans screamed in delight and disbelief for over a minute. Sam wrestled the ball away from the fan and held it up in the air as he climbed back into the park.

JACK ROOSEVELT ROBINSON the first Negro

to enter organized ball, was also one of the greatest infielders ever to play the game. A fiery competitor and a dedicated team-player, he inspired his teammates and demoralized the opposition. Robinson set no great records as a hitter, a base-runner, or a fielder. But no man since Ty Cobb's day could stir such excitement by his very presence on the basepaths. Always alert, and always on the move, he unsettled many a pitcher by his daring fakes and blazing take-offs. He brought back into baseball one of its most thrilling features, the head-long steal of home. Robinson was a solid and authoritative hitter. In his best year (1949) he batted .342. But there was no percentage in a pitcher's walking him to get at a weaker batter, for Robinson, once he stood on base, threatened to come all the way around.

Robinson reached big league baseball rather late in life, via the Kansas City Monarchs of the Negro league, and Montreal of the International League. One of the most popular men ever to play for Montreal, Robinson was almost 30 years old when he finally graduated to the Brooklyn Dodgers in 1947. With Brooklyn he played every infield position, as well as the outfield. His very presence in the line-up seemed enough to raise the team to new heights of accomplishment, for he was ready to extend himself at any time to win the game and he transferred his own enthusiasm to his teammates. At bat, he was ready to bunt, to play hit-and-run, to swing for the fences, or even to get hit with the ball (he was hit seven times in one season). His being a Negro naturally attracted more attention to his performance in that day. But he was an extraordinary ballplayer by any lights and earned his position by his inspired, and inspiring, play.

Robinson led the league in stolen bases with 29 in 1947, his first year in the majors. In 1948 he was the top second-baseman in the league on defense. But even when he was not outstripping all others, he was a constant menace to the other side. No one who ever saw him play—rangy, loose-limbed, reckless and determined—will ever forget him.

EDD J. ROUSH the pride of Indiana, was christened with the two D's in his name. Roush (pronounced Rowsh) is one of the few members of the Hall of Fame who played in three major leagues: The outlaw Federal as well as the American and National. Edd is remembered, wherever he played, for his spectacular defensive play and many fans will hold that he is the best outfielder who ever lived. He made an intense study of batters, so he could position himself properly when they came to bat. But his lightning speed enabled him to reach almost anything hit into center field. In Indianapolis, in Newark, in New York, and in Cincinnati he left memories of over-the-shoulder catches, charging shoe-string grabs, and leaping one-handed saves.

His hitting too was steady and strong, despite his habit of moving about in the box and trying to outguess the pitchers. Apparently he often guessed right, for he led the National League in his second season there (1917) with an average of .341 and led it again in 1919 with an average of .321.

Edd's major league career began with the Chicago White Sox, in 1914, after two seasons in the minors. It was in the Federal League, however, that he came into his own. He starred in center field at Indianapolis and Newark, and when the league collapsed he was picked up, along with Manager

Edd Roush played in
three major leagues
and made great catches in
all of them.

Bill McKechnie, by the New York Giants. They quickly traded him to Cincinnati and he stayed there for ten seasons. He returned then to the Giants for 3 seasons and, after he had stayed home for a whole year rather than accept a salary he thought inadequate, he was allowed to sign again with the Reds and finished his active career with them in 1931.

Roush had been noted as a hold-out even before he stayed home for a season. But it was not always salary that prompted him. He was an abstemious man, always in good condition, and he felt that long spring training wasted both his time and money. No matter how late he reported, it never took him more than a few days to get into playing shape.

GEORGE HERMAN RUTH hit so many home runs

in his major league career (714) that some fans forget that he could do everything well on a baseball diamond. He had a fine throwing arm, made many a circus catch in the outfield, ran the bases with skill, speed, and determination, and was one of the best sliders in the business. And first of all he was a left-handed pitcher, one of the finest who ever pitched for the Boston Red Sox. In 1916, he led the American League pitchers with an earned-run average of 1.75. He pitched 3 World Series games—1 in 1916 and 2 in 1918— and won them all. He set the all-time record at the same time for pitching consecutive scoreless World Series innings (29⅔), a record which stood until 1961. At first base, he was deft as a dancer; and when he first played baseball—at an industrial school for wayward boys—he was the catcher, and not even a right-handed glove that he had to remove before he could throw kept him from being the best in his small circuit.

But of course it was as a hitter that Ruth earned his greatest fame and made his deepest impression on the game. Almost alone he awoke the baseball world to the box-office value of the home run. He not only caused the Yankee Stadium to be built, he caused many a ball club to redesign its park to make home runs more frequent. He changed batting styles from the sandlots to the majors, as every man who came to the plate began to swing the full length of the bat and to try to put every pitch over the fence. He also prompted the

Baseball never saw
a man to equal Babe Ruth
as a personality and
as a player.

Above, Babe Ruth,
standing, left, poses at
contract signing with Red Sox
brass: Owner Harry Frazee,
seated, right;
Secretary Ed Barrow, left.

Ruth hits his first of two homers
against Philadelphia, April 12, 1932,
to open his 19th season. Gehrig
also hit two in this game.

At the close of his career,
Babe often played first base.
He had been a great
pitcher, too.

Babe Ruth, wearing his famous
number 3 for the last time,
accepts Stadium ovation
two months before his death.

doctoring of the ball, to increase its "jack-rabbit" quality, that has caused spasmodic controversy ever since.

Babe Ruth, who was always called "Jidge" by his playmates (Jidge is the New England diminutive for George), was surely the most famous player the professional game ever knew. His name and face were recognized around the world by men and women who would not have understood a box score or known how to hold a bat. Long after he had left the game, he was still a box-office attraction and today his name lives on in the Babe Ruth leagues, where boys in cities throughout the land learn to play organized baseball.

Whether Ty Cobb and Honus Wagner were greater players than Ruth no one can really say. Ruth played his type of baseball better than any other man who ever lived. And there is no denying that his fame, his influence, even his salaries and his dissipations, outstripped those of all other baseball players before or since.

When Ruth entered baseball, right out of the industrial school, he became a pitcher for the Baltimore Orioles in the International League. A skinny, moon-faced boy with a very large head and long legs, he looked little like the gargantuan figure that eventually would win recognition at every way station in the world. In his first spring at Baltimore, in 1914, Ruth pitched an exhibition game against the World Champion Athletics and beat them, and he opened his professional career soon afterward by pitching a shutout against Buffalo. He never hit a single home run for Baltimore (except in exhibition games). He was, instead, one of the fastest left-handed pitchers in the league. In July he was purchased by the Boston Red Sox and farmed to Providence, in the same league as Baltimore. With Providence, where he occasionally played first base, Babe hit his only minor league home run. He won 22 games in the International League that year, and also won 2 games in the American League for the Red Sox. Next year, he was top pitcher on the Red Sox staff. He continued to pitch regularly all the time he was with Boston, although he more and more frequently moved to the outfield until by 1919, when he broke the home-run record with 29 four-baggers in a season, he pitched in only 17 of the 130 games he played. In 1920, he was sold to the Yankees for $100,000, and from that time forth he was the game's greatest hitter. He set a new home-run record immediately, by getting 54 in 142 games. Next year he broke the record again, with 59, and 6 years later, at the age of 32, he set the all-time record of 60 in 154 games. He wound up his career in 1935 with the Boston Braves, after refusing to play again for the Yankees unless he was made manager. Playing first base for the Braves, and serving as assistant manager, Babe faded badly at the plate. He got into only 28 games and hit only 6 home runs. But 3 of them came on the same day, in Forbes Field, Pittsburgh, in a game against the Pirates. And his last one—the last he would ever hit—was, some fans recall, the longest ball ever hit at that park.

ALOYSIUS HARRY SIMMONS (Szymanski) was
known throughout the baseball world in his day as the man who hit with one foot "in the bucket"—that is, with his forward foot striding toward third base rather than toward the pitcher. This stance was supposed to keep a man from ever becoming a good hitter. But it had no such effect on Al.

Raised in Milwaukee, Al wanted to become a professional ballplayer from the time he could understand the game. He led the American League in batting only twice, in 1930 and 1931, with averages of .381 and .390. But he was always among the leaders and earned a major league average of .334, with a high mark of .392 in 1927, when Harry Heilmann led the league with an average of .398.

Al could hit the ball far as well as frequently. On July 15, 1932, he hit 3 home runs in one game. In the fourth game of the 1929 World Series he went to bat twice in the seventh inning, opening it with a home run and then hitting a single when he appeared again, scoring the first and the ninth run in this 10-run inning. But he had done something like that once before: on June 15, 1925, in a game against Cleveland, he hit a single the first time up in the eighth inning and hit a home run when he came to the plate again in the same inning.

Al Simmons (left), was called "Foot-in-the-bucket," but he really kept front foot free to hit to any field.

George Sisler (above), deemed the most graceful fielder in the game, started out as a pitcher and became a topnotch batter.

He began and ended his career with the Philadelphia Athletics, having played 20 seasons in both major leagues.

GEORGE HAROLD SISLER a left-hander, had a
natural advantage at first base and at the plate. He led American League first basemen in assists 6 times—and once led the National League too.

Only Ty Cobb ever earned as high a season's batting average in the American League as George Sisler did when he hit .420 in 1922. (Cobb made his mark 11 years earlier.) In 1920, Sisler had posted a league-leading mark of .407 and that year he established the all-time major league record for total hits in a season: 257.

Sisler was a graceful performer at the plate and in the infield, where he played first base for the St. Louis Browns and the Boston Braves (with a few games for the Washington Senators). He was swift on the basepaths and owned a strong and cunning arm.

He started out in baseball as a college pitcher. In his first year with St. Louis, Sisler won 4 out of 9 games as a pitcher and batted .285. The next year he stopped pitching and hit .305, and never again in his major league career (which was interrupted for a full season by eye trouble) did he drop below that figure for a season's work.

Sisler was a batter in the tradition of Willie Keeler—ready to hit to all fields, to bunt if he found the infield playing deep, or to use a "Baltimore chop" if they tried to anticipate a bunt. He was extremely fast, and batting left-handed as he did, he was able to turn many a bunt into a base hit. But he could hit the ball hard too and one year (1920), just after Babe Ruth had broken all records with his amazing (for that day) total of 29 home runs, Sisler collected 19.

WILLIAM HAROLD TERRY who was born in
Atlanta, Georgia, was a New York Giant for his entire major league career. Bill was a scientific hitter. He batted left-handed and was ready to hit to any field. He took a business-like attitude toward baseball, and he studied the job of hitting. In his 12 full seasons with the Giants he fell below .300 only

once, in 1926, when he was on the bench a good part of the time. In 1930, he hit .401, and in more than 30 years no other National Leaguer has reached that magic mark.

Bill's cold-bloodedness was notorious, thanks to the sports writers who found him difficult to deal with. He was not interested in being "popular" or "colorful." He seldom showed any excitement or strain. He just performed his job in a tenacious, determined way, never slacking, never loafing, never showing off.

Terry began to play ball in Texas, as a pitcher and outfielder. But he was too good a hitter to stay out of the line-up and when McGraw found him in Memphis he determined to make the young man a first baseman. After Terry signed with the Giants he was farmed out to Toledo, where he made an intensive study of his new first-base job. When he came up to the Giants he seemed like a veteran in the position.

When McGraw stepped down as manager in 1932, it was Bill Terry who took over, delighting McGraw with his crafty strategy in the 1933 World Series, after Terry had won his first pennant. But Terry never won another World Series, although he put his team into 2 more. His strategy never really compensated for the lack of his own heavy bat or for the lack of inspiration his own dogged play provided.

HAROLD JOSEPH TRAYNOR called Pie, was
raised in Somerville, Massachusetts, where he was a school hero in football and baseball. He wanted most of all to play baseball for the Boston Braves. The Braves had a scout who lived near young Traynor and the scout urged him to go to Braves Field and work out. But when Traynor got there, the Braves manager, George Stallings, ran him out of the place without even giving him a trial and told him not to come back. This was in 1918, when Pie was 18 years old. Unfortunately for the Braves, Pie Traynor did come back 2 years later, as third baseman for the Pittsburgh Pirates, and kept on coming back (except for 1 year in Birmingham) every year of the next 17.

In Pittsburgh he became the best third baseman of his day, a man whom John McGraw called "the greatest team player

Bill Terry (left), made a
business of baseball.
But he always wanted to win.

Pie Traynor (above), one
of the biggest third basemen,
was a speedster too.

in baseball." Traynor was an even-tempered, self-effacing man who was put out of a ball game only once in his career. But he was a demon competitor who could do everything well. Big for a third baseman (6 feet 1), he was rangy and fast and owned the strongest arm of his era. He could steal ground balls from the shortstop, spear line drives at the baseline, pluck fouls out of the stand, scoop bunts on the run and rifle the ball to first.

Traynor could wallop the ball too. He hit .366 for Pittsburgh in 1930 and had 9 other seasons when he hit over .300. In 1923, when he hit .338, he made 12 home runs and tied for the league leadership in three-baggers (19). In that same year he also topped all third basemen in putouts and assists.

Traynor became manager of the Pirates in 1934, managed from the bench in 1936, came back to play 5 games in 1937, and retired from baseball in 1939, when he was almost 40.

ARTHUR CHARLES VANCE was 29 years old by the time he made the grade in the major leagues. He had failed in three previous attempts to catch on. Finally, Dazzy (he called himself "the Dazzler," but the name, like so many baseball nicknames, was a babyhood pet name) posted 18 wins for Brooklyn in 1922 and led the league with 134 strikeouts. He led the league for the next 6 seasons in that department, attaining a high mark of 262 in 1924, when he was voted the Most Valuable Player in the league.

Vance's irreverent attitude and his easy sense of humor, along with his tremendous speed and willingness to use it, made him a great favorite in Brooklyn, where he fit in with the eccentric crew that earned themselves a dozen different nicknames to indicate that they were all a little touched in the head. Vance organized the "0 for 4" club, of teammates who achieved a perfect zero in 4 trips to the plate.

But on the pitching mound, with his loose underwear shirt flapping, his red face pouring sweat, and his tremendous bulk thrown behind every pitch, Vance was no joke to the opposition. He won 28 games for Brooklyn in 1924 and 22 in 1925, the season in which he pitched his only no-hitter, against Philadelphia on September 13. In his big year, 1924, he once

Dazzy Vance was almost 30 by the time he reached the big leagues.

struck out 7 men in a row. In a 10-inning game against St. Louis in 1925, Vance struck out 17 batters.

PAUL GLEE WANER

a short, wiry young man when he started in baseball, was but 5 feet 8 inches tall and weighed a little more than 150 pounds all his career. At the bat, however, he was too big for most pitchers and they named him Big Poison. (Little Poison was his brother Lloyd, younger and even smaller.)

His merry middle name and the fact that he was born in a place named "Harrah" (Oklahoma) were well suited to Paul Waner's nature. He enjoyed life and he enjoyed baseball and was a popular companion. He liked late hours and good times but better still he liked to help his team win ball games. Paul was a team player who was concerned not so much with his average as with his getting the hit the team needed in a pinch. He had a habit of fouling off good pitches, when a hit was not vital, so that a pitcher might be misled into feeding him that same pitch when there were men on base who had to be brought in. A remarkably sharp-eyed man, he might have posted batting averages as high as any ever registered had he not been so concerned with winning ball games.

Still, Paul did lead the National League 3 times during his 15 seasons with the Pittsburgh Pirates. In his first year with the Pirates he led the league in triples—the speedboys' specialty—and the next year he led in hits, triples, runs batted in, and in batting average.

He ended his career finally in 1946, with Miami, Florida, where he batted .325 in 62 games. But before he quit the majors, while he was still with the Boston Braves in 1942, Waner got the hit he wanted most—his 3000th in the big leagues, to become the only modern National Leaguer, besides Honus Wagner, to achieve that mark. (Stan Musial has now also joined this distinguished group.)

Paul Waner, called "Big Poison," gets his 3000th hit with Braves.

PHOTO CREDITS

8-9 Boston Public Library / 10 New York Public Library, Brown Brothers / 11 New York Public Library, UPI / 12-13 Boston Public Library / 16 New York Public Library / 17 Boston Public Library, New York Public Library / 19 Boston Public Library / 21 Boston Public Library / 22-23 Boston Public Library / 25 Boston Public Library / 26 Boston Public Library / 28 UPI, Brown Brothers / 30 Boston Public Library / 32 Boston Public Library / 33 New York Historical Society / 35 Brown Brothers / 38 Boston Public Library / 39 New York Historical Society, Brown Brothers, Boston Public Library / 41 Boston Public Library / 42 Boston Public Library / 43 Boston Public Library / 46 Boston Public Library / 47 Brown Brothers / 48-49 UPI / 51 Brown Brothers / 52-53 UPI / 56 Brown Brothers / 57 Boston Public Library / 58 Boston Public Library / 59 Boston Public Library / 62 Brown Brothers, Wide World / 63 Boston Public Library / 66 UPI / 67 Brown Brothers / 68 Brown Brothers / 69 Brown Brothers / 71 Brown Brothers / 72 Brown Brothers / 73 Brown Brothers / 75 Boston Public Library / 76 Brown Brothers / 77 Brown Brothers / 79 Boston Public Library / 81 Boston Public Library / 82 Wide World / 83 European / 84-85 New York Public Library / 86 UPI / 88 San Francisco Giants / 89 UPI / 92 Boston Public Library / 93 UPI / 96-97 Wide World / 100 Wide World / 101 Brown Brothers, UPI / 103 Wide World / 104 Brown Brothers / 105 UPI / 108 Brown Brothers, UPI / 109 Brown Brothers / 111 Brown Brothers / 113 Brown Brothers / 114 Brown Brothers / 117 Brown Brothers, UPI / 118 Brown Brothers / 120 Brown Brothers / 121 Brown Brothers / 124 Brown Brothers / 125 UPI / 128 European / 130 European / 131 Brown Brothers / 133 Brown Brothers / 134-35 Wide World / 137 UPI, Brown Brothers / 138 Brown Brothers / 139 UPI / 142 UPI / 143 Wide World / 144-45 Wide World / 146 Brown Brothers / 147 Brown Brothers / 150 Brown Brothers / 151 Wide World / 152-53 Brown Brothers / 154-55 Wide World / 156 Wide World / 157 Brown Brothers / 159 Wide World / 161 Brown Brothers / 162 Brown Brothers / 163 Wide World / 164 San Francisco Giants / 165 San Francisco Giants, Wide World / 166 Brown Brothers / 168-69 Brown Brothers / 170 Wide World / 171 Wide World / 174 UPI / 175 Wide World / 178 Brown Brothers / 179 Brown Brothers / 180 Wide World / 181 Wide World / 182 UPI / 183 Wide World / 186 UPI / 187 Brown Brothers / 189 Wide World / 190 Brown Brothers / 191 UPI / 193 UPI / 195 San Francisco Giants / 197 UPI / 199 Brown Brothers / 200 UPI / 201 Wide World / 204 UPI / 206 UPI / 207 Brown Brothers / 208-09 Wide World / 210 UPI / 211 Wide World / 214 UPI / 215 UPI / 218 T. McDonough / 219 UPI / 221 Brown Brothers / 223 Wide World.